Practical Handbooks in Archaeology
No 13

ROMAN SAMIAN POTTERY IN BRITAIN

Peter Webster

With contributions by
G B Dannell

Illustrations by Peter Webster and
Yvonne Beadnell

1996
Council for British Archaeology

It is a well known truism that any teacher learns as much from his students as they do from him. This has certainly been the case with the many who have acted as 'test drivers' of early versions of this booklet during various samian projects in Cardiff and area. It is to them that this booklet is dedicated with my thanks for giving me the opportunity to share an interest in samian with them.

Published 1995 by the Council for British Archaeology
Bowes Morrell House, 111 Walmgate, York, YO1 2UA

British Library Cataloguing in Publication Data
A catalogue card for this book is available from the British Library

ISBN 1 872414 56 7

Typeset by M C Bishop, Chirnside, Berwickshire
Printed by Adpower, Halifax

Contents

Preface

This booklet, although a new production, has a pedigree running back over several years. Its origin lies in material prepared for undergraduate and extramural students of the then University College, Cardiff. It first appeared in booklet form for use in a series of residential courses on samian pottery led by Geoffrey Dannell in the early 1980s.

Although there is an obvious connection between this volume and its three predecessors, it is not a fourth edition. Only parts of the earlier text have been retained and revised, while the order has been completely changed to suit the new format. The work of 'l'équipe Britannique' at La Graufesenque, and of Allard Mees and others elsewhere, make a revision of the South Gaulish figure types advisable and these are omitted here. I am most grateful to Joanna Bird, Geoffrey Dannell, Brenda Dickinson, Brian Hartley, Margaret Ward, and Janet Webster for reading through this new work, and for their many helpful suggestions. Portions of Chapter 2 were originally written by Geoffrey Dannell and I owe a particular debt to him both for allowing me to use these as I choose and for the benefit of discussion on matters concerning samian ware over many years.

Like the earlier booklets, this one has been written in the belief that there is no reason why anyone with an interest in samian should not quickly achieve sufficient competence both to identify forms and to have reasonable success with the identification of decorative schemes. It has been prepared in the hope that more people will take an active interest in samian. It is intended as a work to be used, and I hope that it will find its way into the finds shed (and onto the site director's table), as well as into other places where samian is stored. As with all pottery, the more samian you can handle the more you learn about it — and the more you realise what you do not know. Neither this nor the considerable samian literature should, however, put off any archaeologist, whether 'professional' or 'amateur' from exploring what is not only a fascinating subject, but also an essential dating tool on many sites.

PVW
Cardiff 1994

1 Introduction

The purpose of this work is to provide an introduction to samian ware in Britain. The aim is essentially a practical one: to provide sufficient information to allow those handling samian, whether in an excavation or a museum context, to establish the approximate date range of the material, and to assess the quality of information which it might yield.

To do this, it will be necessary to look at the way in which samian was made, as in this lies the key to understanding the reasoning behind divisions into 'plain' and 'decorated' samian, and that which lies behind the methods used to analyse decorative schemes.

The emphasis, where possible, will be on Britain, but the wide distribution of samian means that continental material is always important and ensures that samian has an extensive and multilingual literature, which can be very daunting, particularly to a British audience. A major aim is, therefore, to provide a key to the available literature.

The term 'samian ware' is now commonly used in English to describe a variety of red-gloss pottery made mainly in Gaul and Germany, and exported to Britain from the mid 1st to the mid 3rd century. In its Latin form, the term seems to have been used by the Romans to signify almost all red pottery with the same disregard for the obvious geographical implications of the term, as is found in our present day use of the word 'china'. Continental archaeologists tend to use the term 'terra sigillata', or derivatives with scarcely more regard for the literal meaning of the words.

In fact, samian ware was just one product of a series of manufacturing centres, nearly all of which made other ceramics. The origins of samian lie in the techniques of Greek slip-decorated pottery (including black and red figured ware) and its Hellenistic successors, including Italian black-slipped wares (the so-called 'Campanian black-glazed' ware) and moulded bowls. These constitute the common ancestors of a large number of Roman slipped wares made by industries in various parts of the Empire. The immediate ancestor of the Gaulish industry was the red slipware industry of north central Italy, centred on Arezzo in Tuscany. The techniques (but only some of the artistic 'flair') of the Arretine potters were transferred to Gaul, where, from c AD 25, mass production was centred at La Graufesenque at the southern end of the Massif Central, near present-day Millau (Aveyron). From here,

1

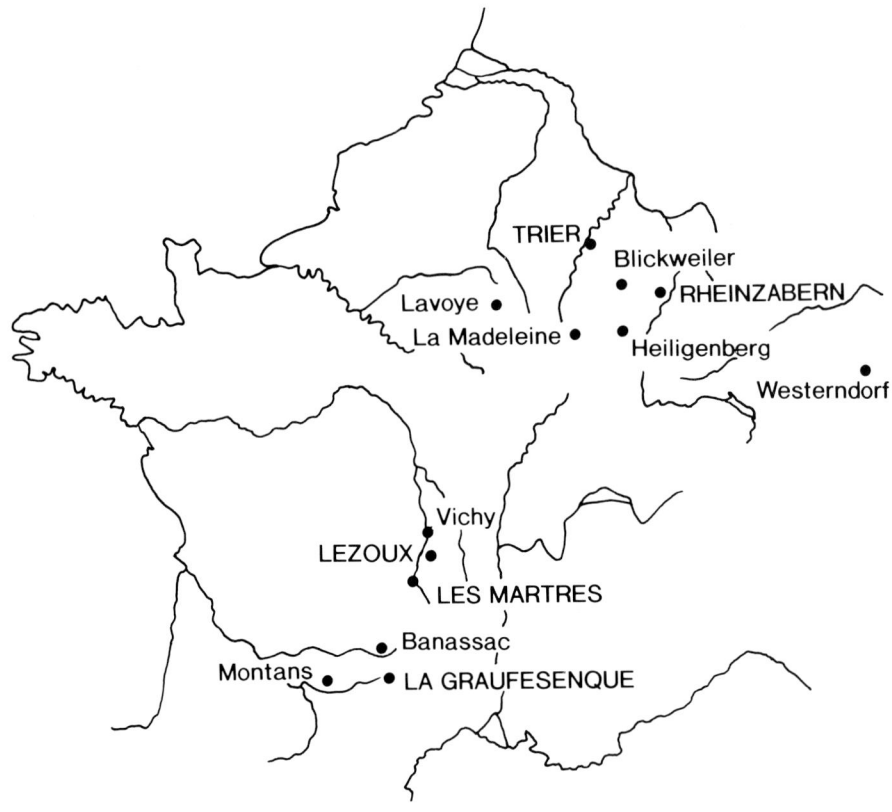

Fig 1 Samian manufacturing sites

South Gaulish samian ware was exported, probably by mule-train, to the Mediterranean coast, at, or near, Narbonne and thence, presumably by water transport, to markets in the western Mediterranean, Germany, and (from the early 40s AD) Britain.

The South Gaulish centres flourished throughout much of the 1st century, with little apparent competition from similar products. By the late 1st century, however, it must have been evident to those producing and marketing the ware that the expanding markets of Gaul, Germany and Britain were not most easily served by a centre whose main trade outlet was to the south. Perhaps for this reason we find more northerly production centres proliferating in the 2nd century. Of greatest importance for the trade with Britain were the centres in Central Gaul in an area near present-day

2

Clermont-Ferrand. Here the kilns at Les Martres-de-Veyre exported samian, often of fine quality, mainly within the period c AD 100–120, although, if quantitative studies in Britain are correct, in smaller amounts than South Gaul. The Les Martres production overlaps with what may be seen as a terminal decline in the South Gaulish industry, the main exporting period of which is generally thought to have ended by c AD 110. Late South Gaulish samian is characterized by a marked decline in both artistic and production standards, and it looks as if the main impetus for Gaulish samian production shifted north around the turn of the century.

The dominance of Les Martres-de-Veyre in the British market was, however, short lived. About 120, the potters of nearby Lezoux, after several generations of experimentation and limited output, started producing 'export-quality' samian which quickly captured the British market and retained the lion's share of it until the sudden, and not entirely explained, demise of Lezoux export in the late 2nd century.

The expansion of samian production was not, however, yet complete. Throughout the 2nd century a whole host of centres started up in the Argonne and in the valleys of the Moselle and the Rhine. These centres, collectively known as 'East Gaulish', were primarily concerned with the local and German markets. The major trade artery of the Rhine did, however, provide them with an easy route to Britain and East Gaulish ware is found in small but significant amounts, particularly in eastern Britain, from late Hadrianic times until the decline of East Gaulish production in the mid 3rd century.

2 The manufacture of samian ware

Archaeological reports tend to divide samian into 'plain' and 'decorated' forms. This is not only an archaeological convenience but reflects two different methods of production.

Plain ware

Plain samian forms seem to have been made on the potters' wheel with the aid of shaped burnishing tools, or perhaps with templates. The curved diagonal lines sometimes visible on the walls of vessels may be a sign of these processes, but more indicative is the difference in surface treatment in open and closed vessels. All surfaces on open vessels (bowls, dishes, etc) are smooth, but the interior surfaces of closed vessels (jars, flagons etc) display the familiar finger-rilling of wheel-thrown vessels, something never seen on surfaces which could be 'mechanically' smoothed. A possible arrangement of mechanical aids for use in the manufacture of plain ware is shown by Czysz (1982).

After the initial manufacture of the basic vessels, footrings were shaped (or, in some forms, added), together with decorative details. Some of the latter were trailed *en barbotine* using a trailed slip technique much like that used to decorate a cake with icing. Leaves and even figures could be added in this way. Other vessels had impressed designs made by roulette wheels, while a few forms had added strap handles. Mortaria of form 45 had a lion-head spout added pre-formed from a small mould.

Once complete, vessels were allowed to dry to leather-hardness on boards or mats, and were then dipped in a slip which appears to have been a refined and liquid version of a clay, which ensured a good thermal match for the firing process. To avoid the sticky wet slip glueing the unfired vessels down as they dried, the footrings were placed on sanded surfaces. The sand adhering to the footrings further prevented vessels sticking to each other when stacked in the kiln for firing. Particles of sand can often be seen on the fired footrings, and also on the upper basal surface where stacking in the kiln has impressed sand from the footring of an adjacent vessel.

Probably as a result of the method of manufacture, which favours a repetitive process, a relatively small number of shapes were current at any one time, and an even smaller number were particularly popular. This situation lends itself to classification by form, and this is the basis for the study of plain ware.

Decorated ware

As noted above, plain ware could be decorated using barbotine or roulettes. But those vessels usually categorized as 'decorated samian' were made using moulds.

Before production of moulded samian could begin, the moulds themselves had to be made. Mould-making involved several related components:

1 *A basic mould shape* would be made using a fine-grained clay thrown on a wheel and smoothed internally to take a series of decorative designs impressed into the interior while the clay was still plastic.
2 *Individual stamps* (or punches) used to produce decorative details were, for the most part carved from plastic clay. The representations are in positive relief and frequently display considerable artistic skill. The French word *poinçon* is given generically to these punches.

   Favourite details were copied and recopied, either by eye, by taking an impression from a mould, or by moulding from a finished bowl (*surmoulage*) and, perhaps, by moulding from a master *poinçon*. In all these cases, fine details will tend to become obscure, and the standard of the result to degenerate the further one is from the original. Due to the shrinkage of clay on firing, copies will also be smaller than the original.
3 *Styli* were used to scribe borders and the flowing tendrils of scrolls.
4 *Roulettes* could be used for repetitive designs such as an egg-and-tongue frieze (an *ovolo* border) or a bead row, although repeated use of a single *poinçon* is more common than one might expect.

Designs could be laid out in the mould with the aid of compasses, 'spiders' consisting of a fixed number of spikes to mark out the spacing for details or

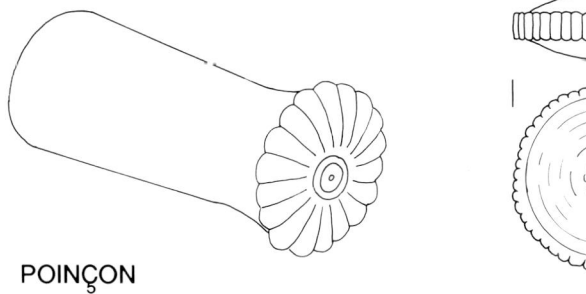

POINÇON   ROULETTE

Fig 2   *Fig 3*

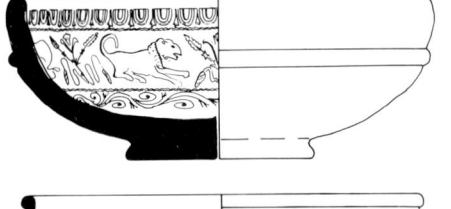

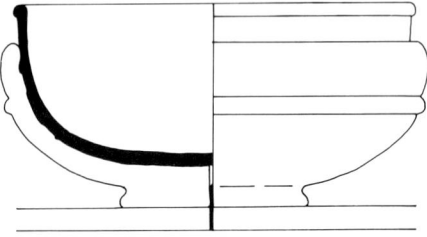

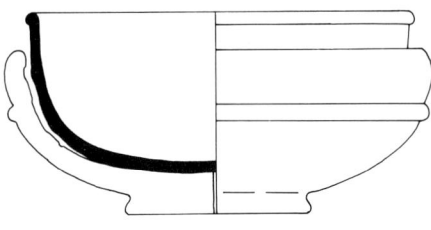

Figure 4 Making a decorated samian bowl

1 The mould was prepared using individual poinçons, roulettes and styli to produce the desired pattern in negative on the inside of the mould. The mould was fired.

2 The mould was fixed to the potter's wheel either by luting with fresh clay or using a peg which engaged in a hole through the centre of the mould base. Clay was placed in the mould and drawn up and pressed into the mould as it rotated on the wheel. The rim was fashioned above the top of the mould and exposed surfaces smoothed.

3 The mould and part-made bowl were left to dry. As the bowl dried, it also shrank away from the mould and so could be removed without damage.

4 The footring of the bowl could then be added (as was usual with form 37) or carved from the base of the moulded bowl (form 29, a few form 37s and some other forms). After drying, the bowl was dipped in slip and left to dry on a sanded surface. When fully dry it was ready for firing. Meanwhile the mould was cleaned and dried ready for further use.

with styli (to provide guide lines), but the experience and 'eye' of the potter was probably the most important factor in achieving a well-spaced layout.

Once he had assembled his equipment and placed any preliminary marks for his design, the potter would have impressed his details into the interior of the mould to give a 'negative' design. The repertoire of details available (the *poinçons* etc) was considerable and could be used in unending combination. The mould was finally dried and fired.

The decorated vessels themselves were produced:

1 By pegging or luting the mould to a wheel and throwing clay within it, raising the vessel and pressing the clay into the moulded detail at the same time.
2 The pressure needed to get good relief may have encouraged the use of mechanical templates.
3 The rim was drawn up above the top of the mould. Both rim and interior would have been smoothed with specially shaped tools (as in the case of plain ware) and the whole set aside to allow the vessel to dry.
4 In drying, the vessel would shrink sufficiently for it to be turned out of the mould without damage.
5 Once the vessel was out of the mould, the footring could be fashioned or applied. The vessel would then go through the drying, slipping and firing process in the same way as plain ware.

Potters and their stamps

One of the most archaeologically valuable aspects of samian is that many of the forms, both decorated and plain, carry impressed names of the workshops and the people who worked in them. On plain vessels these marks usually appear on the basal interior as a central mark. On decorated ware they may occur in a variety of places as indicated on Fig 5.

Stamps may have served a variety of purposes:

1 To help control the quality of the work within a large workshop.
2 To distinguish the work of different potters or workshops when work was fired in common.
3 To act as an 'advertisement' on a decorated vessel. Such stamps are distinguished by their greater size, elaboration and legibility.

In addition, mould makers sometimes signed their work, generally with a stylus, in script or rustic capitals. Such signatures could be written backwards in the mould so as to appear normally on the finished bowl. They are not

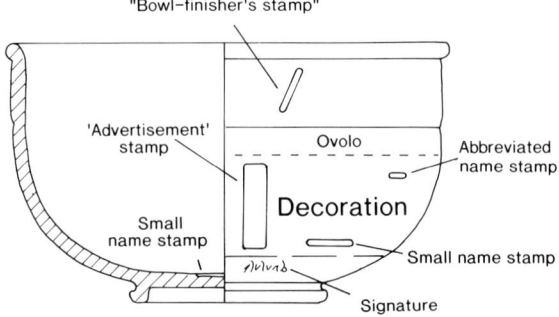

"Bowl-finisher's stamp"

'Advertisement' stamp

Ovolo

Abbreviated name stamp

Small name stamp

Decoration

Small name stamp

Signature

MAKERS' MARKS
Some Possible Positions

Figure 5 Makers' marks. The so-called 'bowl-finisher's stamp' may occur on the rim, as shown, or, occasionally, below the decoration. It presumably belongs to the bowl maker (as opposed to the maker of the mould).

unknown in among the decoration but are often found at the bottom of the mould so that they were frequently cleaned off in finishing or covered by the footring. Small stamps, often those normally used for plain ware, may also occur inserted in the decoration by the mould maker. The 'advertisement' stamps already mentioned are, of course, also placed there by the mould maker.

Other stamps, for instance those in the basal interior of bowls and those on rims, must have been impressed by the bowl maker. On any given bowl, the names represented by the stamp (or stamps) and by the signature, if present, may be the same or may be different. Some mould makers are associated with a number of name-stamps impressed by bowl makers (and so presumably sold to several different makers). Sometimes stamps are found on the plain rim above the decoration. Such stamps are of a type normally found on the interior of plain vessels and could, for instance, indicate a plain ware maker who has bought in moulds to make decorated ware.

A further complicating factor is the occurrence of signatures scratched on moulds *after* firing (sometimes referred to as a signature *post cocturam*) and presumably indicating ownership of the mould. When transferred to the finished bowl, these are difficult in practice to distinguish from mould makers' signatures but close examination of the script may make it possible to

8

distinguish between letters originally written in wet clay and those scratched later.

The terminology used on stamps varies and contains implied information about the workshops involved. The main formulae types are as follows:

1 Use of the term *officina* usually in abbreviation, either as OF, OFIC or OFFIC. The term may be translated as 'workshop' and seems to imply a large firm controlled by the person named. Detailed study of stamps and graffiti from La Graufesenque confirms the usage there; elsewhere it is less certain.

2 Use of the word *fecit* ('made [this]'), either in full or abbreviated to FEC, FE or simply F. This has a more personal feel and suggests a small operation in which the person named made the pots himself.

3 Use of the word *manu* ('by the hand of...'), most commonly abbreviated to M. This again seems to imply a small operation and personal production, but the evidence is not wholly consistent.

4 Use of the potter's name, either in the nominative or in the genitive; eg. BASSUS (Bassus [made this]) or BASSI ([the work] of Bassus). Here, either personal production or a larger workshop could be implied, although small scale personal production seems more likely for the nominative stamps.

The matter is dealt with more extensively by Polak in a preliminary study of the Vechten stamps (Polak 1989).

It must be remembered that the *position* of stamps is also important. Stamps placed in the decoration before firing can generally be taken to imply the name of the potter or the firm making the mould. Those in the basal interior or in plain zones externally give only the name of the potter or firm making that particular pot. This might be the maker of the mould but it is not necessarily so. It is clear that the variety of tasks which go towards making a decorated vessel (*poinçon*-making, mould-making, bowl-making) could involve a division of labour and there is no necessity for the finished bowl to be made by the same firm as the mould (or *poinçon*).

Firing samian

The technology of firing samian seems to have been remarkably similar at all centres. It required the separation of the flue gases containing reducing carbon (which would have turned the pots black) from the firing chamber (in which the pots were stacked) which needed a pure oxidizing atmosphere. This was most frequently achieved by leading the flue gases through closed vertical

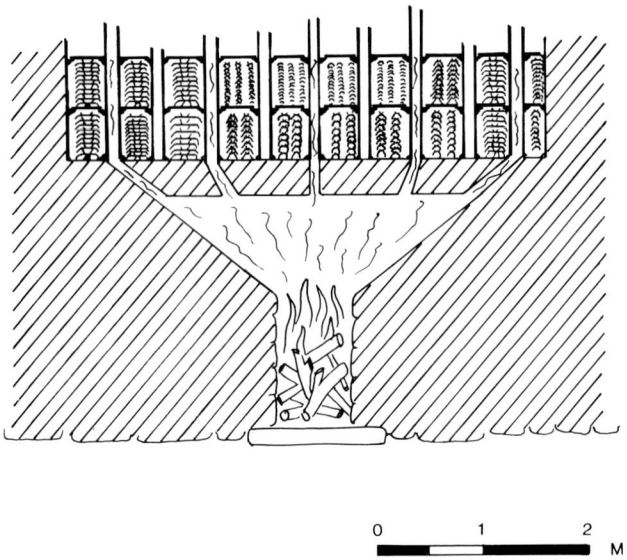

Figure 6 Reconstruction of part of the interior of a samian kiln (after Vernhet 1981). As the stacking of pots proceeded, the interior was built up using prefabricated tubes, supports and floor sections, held together by fresh clay luting. After firing, the luting was broken away as the kiln was demolished. Prefabricated elements could then be used again.

passages, often pottery tubes, up through the chamber itself. In this way, the pots received the heat of the fire without being subjected to its fumes. The oxidizing atmosphere, achieved through a plentiful air supply, was necessary to obtain the fully oxidized (red) colour. Careful control of the kiln conditions is implied by the remarkably uniform nature of the end products, despite the numerous centres and the varying size and shape of known kilns.

The vast majority of the output of the samian potteries was in the red oxidized fabric which we associate with the name 'samian'. It must, however, be remembered that the same pottery centres often produced other classes of pottery of varying degrees of fineness. In addition, variants on the standard samian fabric were occasionally made. These include vessels with a *marbled* slip and the so-called *black samian* which appears to be a standard samian fabric with reduced surface (presumably achieved by altering the kiln atmosphere at the very end of the firing).

Reconstructions of parts of a kiln interior, based on elements found at La

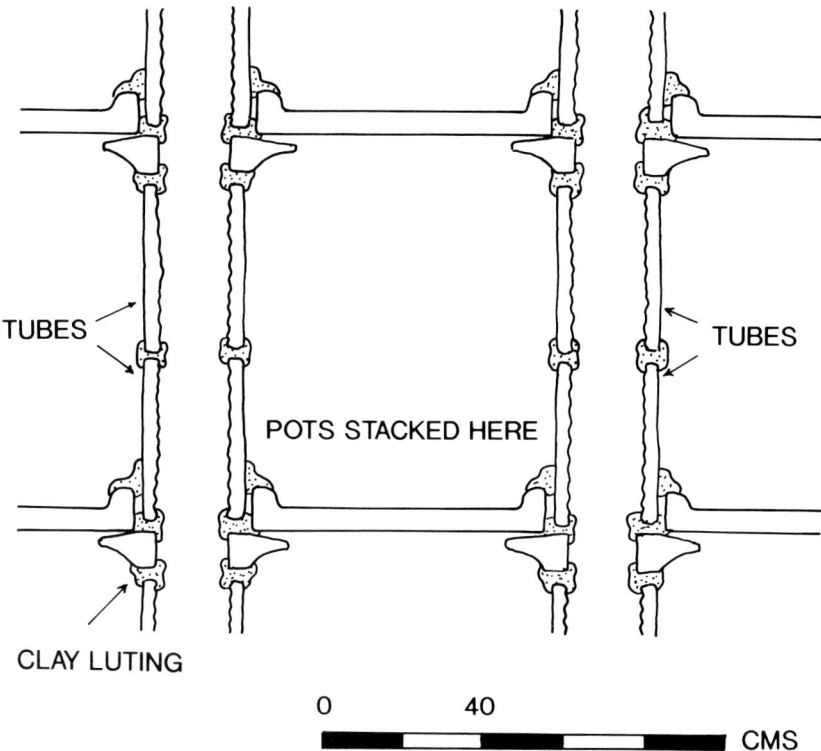

TUBES

TUBES

POTS STACKED HERE

CLAY LUTING

0   40

CMS

Figure 7 Reconstructed cross section of part of a samian kiln (after Vernhet 1981). Heat from the fire passed through holes in the kiln floor directly into the tubes. These conducted it through the oven, providing heat, but not fumes, to the pots stacked there. The prefabricated nature of the tubes, supports and kiln floors is evident.

Graufesenque (see Vernhet 1981), are illustrated as Figs 6–7. The tubes, supports and flooring tiles which make up the major part of the kiln interior appear to have been prefabricated. As the kiln was stacked with pots, the interior would have been built up using the prefabricated elements luted together with fresh clay to seal the joints. At the end of firing the kiln interior would be dismantled and the prefabricated elements cleaned for reuse.

The sizes of samian kilns vary considerably, but some, at least, were capable of firing a very large number of pots at one time and it is clear that the controller of the kiln (called here the 'kiln master') was an important and skilled operator. However, occasionally, accidents did occur in firing, as the stacks of overfired vessels welded together by heat (the so-called *moutons*) attest, and such dangers, along with the large numbers of vessels involved, seem to have induced some potters to contribute to communal firing rather than have kilns dedicated to firing the products of a single workshop.

In the 1st century at La Graufesenque, the kiln master included with the firing a whole vessel which had scratched on it names (presumably of the potters providing work for firing), the types and sizes of vessel, and the relevant quantities (cf Marichal 1988). Complete lists of this type suggest that between 27,000 and 30,000 pots could be fired at one time. When firing was complete, it was obviously necessary to account for the load as recorded (and for losses) and the tally lists presumably fulfilled this requirement. However, many of the names on the kiln tallies are not known as stamps impressed on the vessels themselves and the exact significance for the samian producers of both stamps and tallies remains somewhat obscure. Indeed, it is plain that we are only at the beginning of our understanding of the complex relationships between workers at the various stages of production, and that much patient research is still to be undertaken if we are to get a proper understanding of those involved in the making of samian.

3 Fabrics

Relatively minor variations in the fabrics produced at the various samian centres serve to distinguish one from another. While division by fabric can help in arriving at a date, there are generally more readily distinguishable features (eg form, decoration) which may be more helpful in achieving greater chronological precision. Reliance on fabric alone can be very difficult indeed. However, the following may help to distinguish some of the fabrics of particular centres:

South Gaul (La Graufesenque)

Early La Graufesenque ware tends to have a dull brown coat. However, the fabric more generally seen is, at its best, a highly fired fabric giving conchoidal fractures (ie ripple-like breaks often seen on broken glass) and possessing a good wax-like slip. The slipped surface tends to be dark red or cherry red in colour. In the break, the fabric is pinkish and usually shows numerous white flecks (and sometimes streaks), particularly if viewed through a hand lens. In the late Flavian period, the flecks are often yellowish. Late South Gaulish products deteriorated markedly from the earlier high quality, so that the surface is often much less glossy and there are signs of careless treatment. However, the fabric is usually red (or pinkish in the break) when compared with the products of other centres.

South Gaul (Montans)

This fabric is far less common than that from La Graufesenque. It is generally lighter and often yellowish, although red or pink is not unknown. The slip tends to be browner and more matt than that of La Graufesenque.

Central Gaul (Les Martres-de-Veyre)

The fabric is usually bright red or intense orange-red and dense. The slip usually shows a good satin-like gloss. There are no white flecks in the fabric which generally appears devoid of inclusions to the naked eye (although some will be visible at higher magnification). Vessels can be very carelessly finished, with nail and finger marks and often major blemishes, but, at its best, the finish is smooth and the moulded work crisp.

Central Gaul (Lezoux)

The earliest Lezoux fabrics appear only rarely in Britain. They use non-calcareous clays and are often visibly micaceous and coarse-textured with a brown, orange or red slip.

The main export period (from c AD 120) produced fabrics which generally appear more brown or orange-brown in comparison with the redder South Gaulish fabrics. Slips are usually more 'grainy', lacking the wax-like gloss of South Gaul at its best. Fabrics, although hard, were not fired to a temperature which would produce conchoidal fractures. In the break, the fabric commonly shows some mica, if examined with a hand lens, and appears more mixed and granular than South Gaulish or Les Martres fabrics. It can contain white specks (as do South Gaulish fabrics) but other inclusions are also noticeable.

East Gaul

Fabrics vary according to centre and date. In general, orangey fabric and reddish-orange slips may point to East Gaulish manufacture notably at La Madeleine or in the Argonne. Rheinzabern fabrics are usually particularly red. Trier fabrics tend to be pinker with dense chalk, or similar to Lezoux in colour, but with more chalk and no visible mica. Later products often show a markedly poor standard of decoration and of detail, but some forms, such as the incised jars, beakers and cups (O&P, pl LXXVII–LXXVIII), are usually very fine and carefully made. The latest (mid-3rd century) fabrics of Trier and Rheinzabern are often pale pink or yellowish, sometimes with thin, pale and matt slips.

Later (late 3rd or 4th century) Argonne wares can occur in Britain and are similar to earlier Argonne samian in fabric. Where decorated with roller stamps (eg Gose 1984, type 18) they will be easily distinguishable, but caution is needed with small undiagnostic sherds.

General

It will be seen that most of the characteristics mentioned above are not so much absolute as comparative, arrived at by comparing fabrics from the various centres with each other. Generally the best method of distinguishing the fabric of a particular sherd is to place it beside examples of fabrics from known centres. Here fragments which can be identified as products of specific centres on the basis of their moulded detail or stamps are, of course, crucial. For details of fabric analysis see Picon et al 1971; 1975, and Picon 1973.

It should be noted that adverse soil conditions (such as those often encountered in upland Britain) can affect both colour and texture. It should also be remembered that the appearance of the pottery may have been affected by events subsequent to its manufacture. Most frequently encountered is samian burnt black by a fire on the site of its deposition.

It is strongly recommended that fabrics are studied in natural light, as artificial light tends to alter colour perception and makes a task, which can be difficult anyway, even more so.

Other centres and other fabrics

The manufacture of samian took place on a large number of sites in Gaul, Germany and Switzerland (and closely related fabrics were also made in Hungary, north Italy and Spain). Many of these centres were of only local importance but (like Lezoux in the 1st century) their products were occasionally exported. Unusual samian fabrics will, therefore, sometimes occur in Britain. There is no easy way to identify such items. However, many of the smaller Gaulish sites are considered in a compendium by Bémont and Jacob (1986). Large site collections already studied for their fabrics (eg London) may be of use in helping to locate other sources.

Samian forms and fabrics were imitated by some British potteries. The more successful potters, producing moulded decorated ware in addition to plain ware, as at Colchester, and the so-called 'Aldgate-Pulborough Potter', can be classed as makers of British samian (see below p 100). More often, the aim was simply to copy the samian shapes. However, some centres went so far as to use red slip on such wares, and the better products of Caerleon and Oxfordshire can look superficially like samian. The so-called 'black samian' (see above p 10) was also imitated in the Nene Valley. In the case of most of these imitations, it is the fabric in the break, rather than the finish, which will distinguish such pieces, but most samian specialists have learnt to expect a few 'non-samian' pieces among samian collections presented to them, just as coarse pottery specialists must expect the occasional atypical samian item.

It should be remembered that the Gaulish samian industry is but one branch of a widespread Roman red slipped tradition, which did not stop with the end of Gallic samian production. In Britain, the Oxfordshire red colour-coated ware (cf Young 1977) is in the Roman red-slipped tradition and some of its forms are close to those found particularly in East Gaulish samian. Usually the coarse, layered structure of the Oxford fabric is sufficient to distinguish it from true samian sherds. Less frequently found are sherds from another red-slipped industry in North Africa. In the main, North African red-slipped pottery appears in different forms from Gaulish samian and the fabric (and slip) tends to look more granular. For further details and a catalogue of forms and fabrics found in Britain, see Bird 1977. For a review of this class of pottery as a whole, see Hayes 1972 and 1980.

4 Classification

Samian has been classified by a number of writers. The forms proposed by Dragendorff, Déchelette, Knorr, and Walters form a continuous numerical sequence (Dragendorff forms 1–55, Déchelette forms 56–77, Knorr form 78, and Walters forms 79–81). In this work, this series will generally be referred to simply as 'form...'. Forms derived from the separate classifications of Ludowici, Curle and Ritterling will always be preceded by the names of their authors.

In this section, we are primarily concerned with assisting readers in the classification of vessels or sherds from excavations *in Britain*. Details of forms classified numerically and with their dating and main characteristics will be found below as follows:

> The Dragendorff-Déchelette-Knorr-Walters series on pp 29–65.
> Additional types found in the Curle series on pp 66–67.
> Those from the Ludowici series on pp 68–69.
> Those from the Ritterling series on pp 70–72.
> Those identified by Oswald and Pryce and others on pp 67, 69 and 73.

As a brief introductory guide, a summary 'visual index' follows. This divides vessels according to whether they are decorated (ie mould-decorated) or 'plain'. Plain wares are further divided according to their class, so that all bowls appear together, as do all cups, all mortaria, etc. It is worth remembering that rouletting and barbotine decoration can occur on 'plain' forms and moreover that even decorated vessels have plain areas. The rims of form 37 and the basal area of form 30 can be large, are undecorated, and are frequently found broken from the remainder of the vessel.

The 'visual index' is not intended as a substitute for the fuller discussion in the catalogue which follows it. It is merely a key into the catalogue, where common variations and diagnostic details will be found along with discussion, dating, and bibliography.

It is an obvious point but one worth bearing in mind, that the Roman potters had not heard of Dragendorff and they were not consciously following a classification, but producing the shapes that they thought they could sell (just as their modern counterparts produce tea-cups, plates, etc). The determining of a form number within a classification such as this should not, therefore, be an end in itself but only a means to an end – generally the acquiring of information likely to help determine the chronological, economic, or social history of a particular site.

Visual index

The divisions within this index are designed as responses to simple questions or to meet simple criteria:

1 Is the vessel decorated, ie made mainly with the aid of a decorated mould, or plain, ie made mainly without a mould? Remember that portions of plain forms may be rouletted, decorated *en barbotine*, or even, as in the case of form 45 spouts, decorated using a small subsidiary mould. Decorated vessels appear on Figs 8–9, plain vessels on Figs 10–16.
2 If plain, is it a cup or small bowl/dish (Fig 10), a bowl (Fig 11), dish (Fig 12), or plate or wide dish (Fig 13), or a mortarium or mortar-like bowl (Fig 14)?
3 Some plain forms clearly belonged to larger 'sets', which included bowls and cups/dishes of similar form but different size. The commoner groups are illustrated in Fig 15.
4 Most closed vessels sherds encountered will be from decorated jars/beakers. There are, however, a few undecorated closed vessels, some of which are illustrated in Fig 16.

Once a form is found in the visual index, details can be found in the catalogue (p 28 ff). If a vessel does not appear to be in the index, then it is probably best to seek approximations to it in the catalogue as obviously, all variations of rim form etc are not covered in the index. The catalogue also gives bibliographical details of other sources of information and these may include variations. If all of these fail, then the vessel may be an unusual form, and suggestions as to procedure are to be found on p 73.

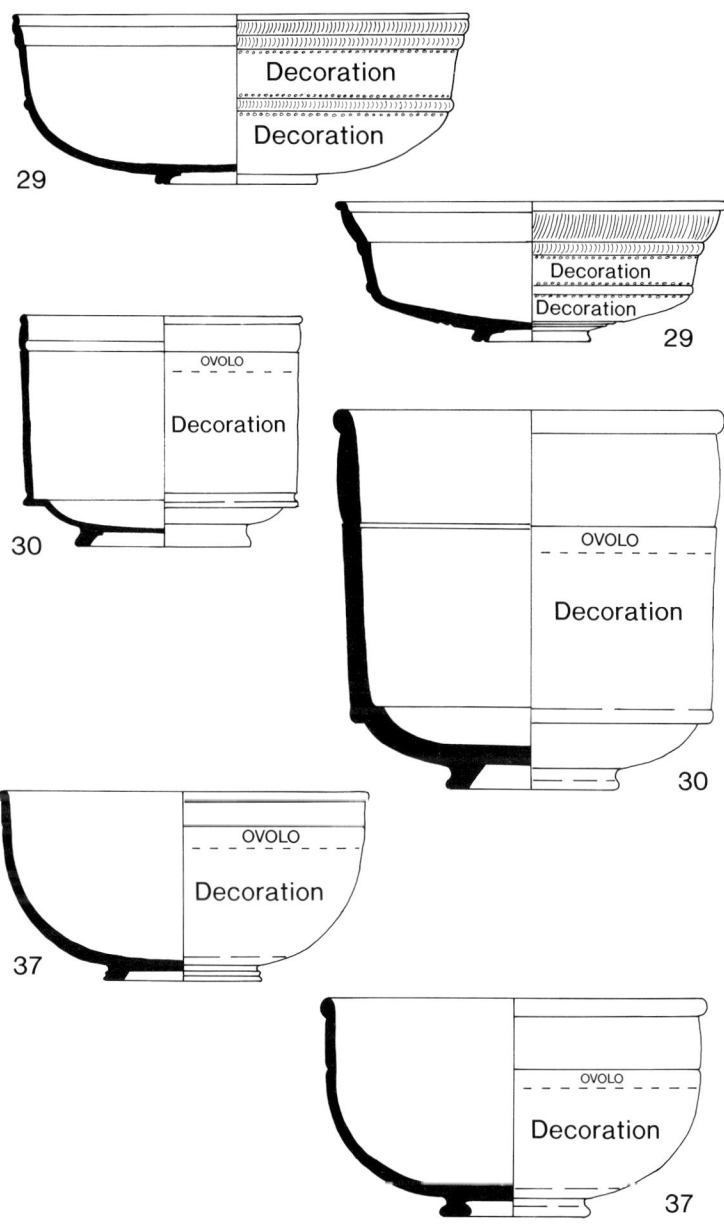

Fig 8 *The more common decorated bowls*

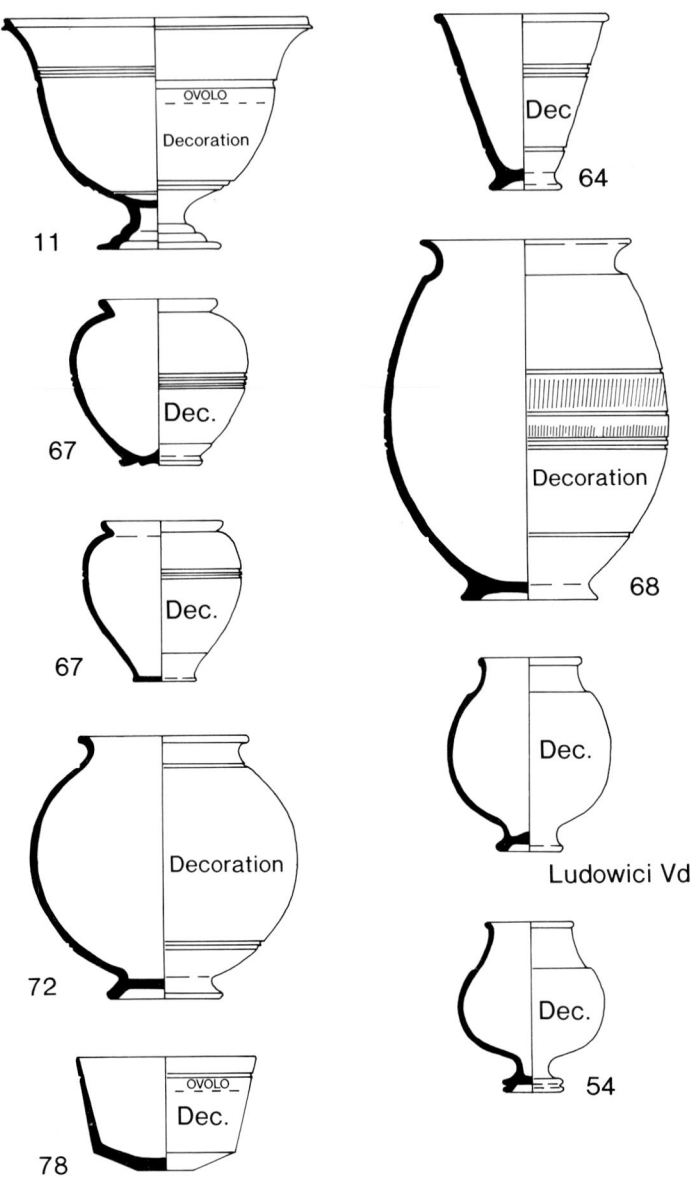

Fig 9 The less common decorated vessels

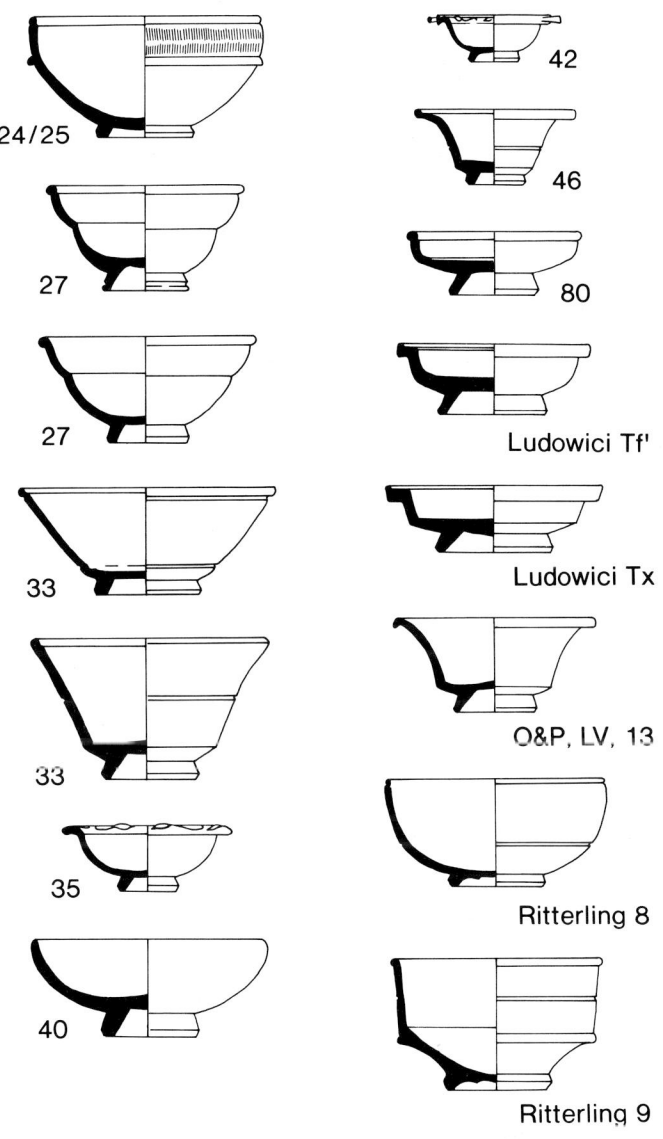

24/25

27

27

33

33

35

40

42

46

80

Ludowici Tf'

Ludowici Tx

O&P, LV, 13

Ritterling 8

Ritterling 9

Fig 10 Cups and small bowls

21

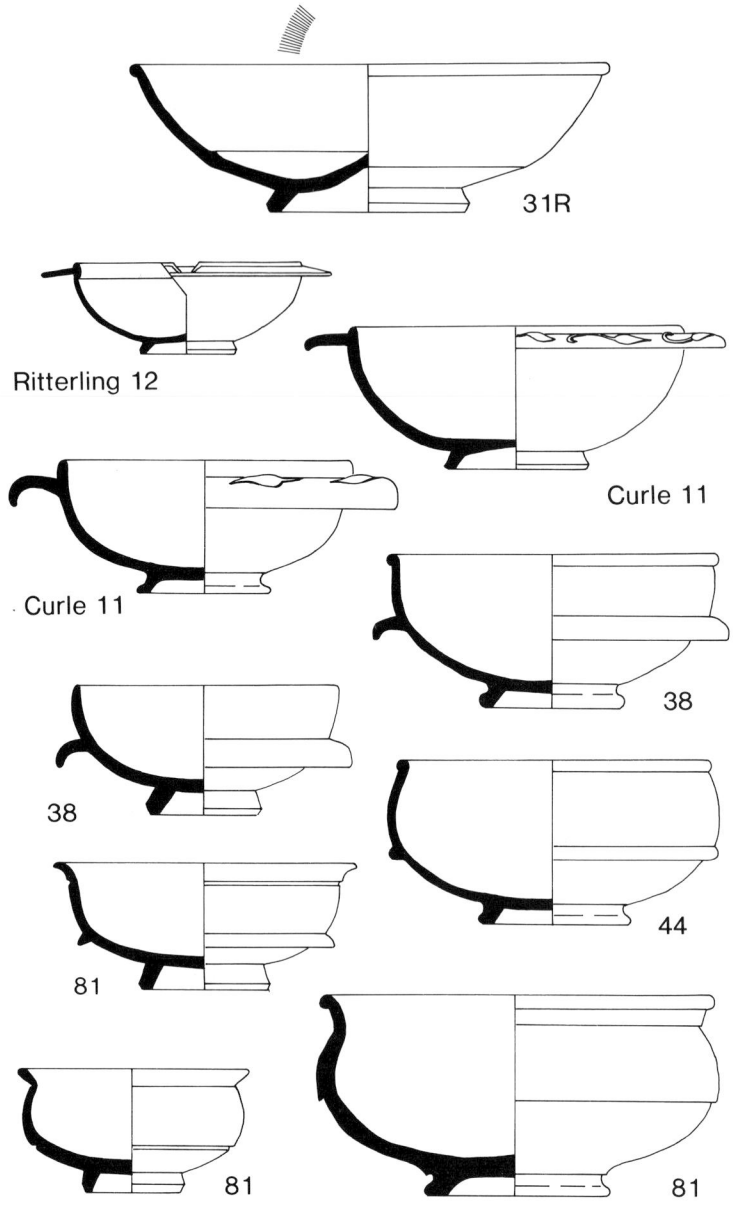

31R

Ritterling 12

Curle 11

Curle 11

38

38

44

81

81

81

Fig 11 Bowls

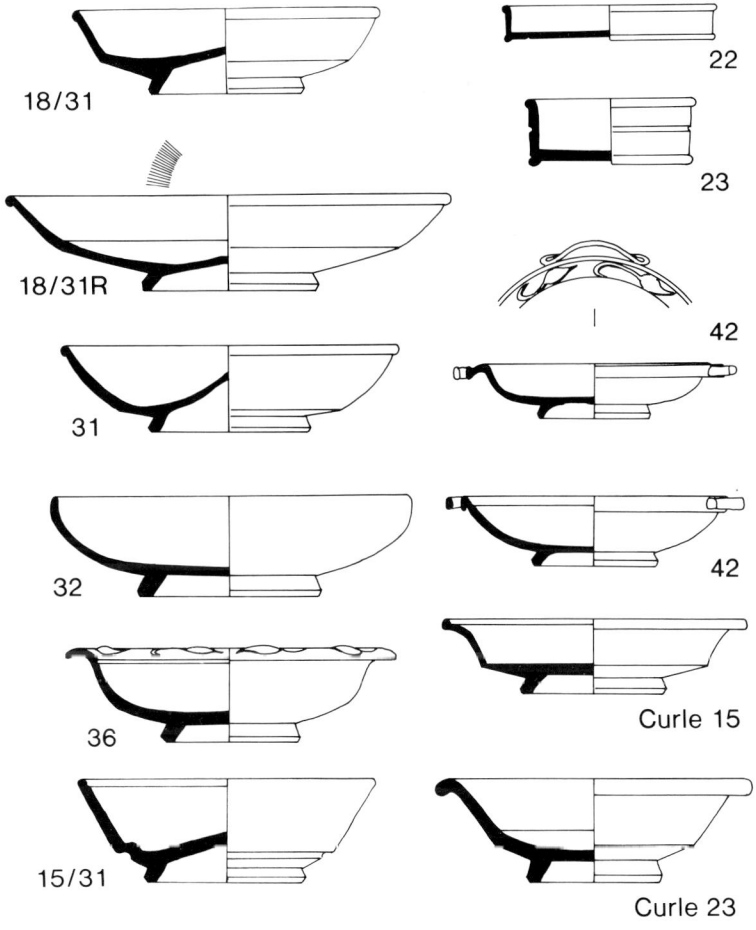

18/31

22

23

18/31R

42

31

42

32

Curle 15

36

15/31

Curle 23

Fig 12 Dishes and shallow bowls

23

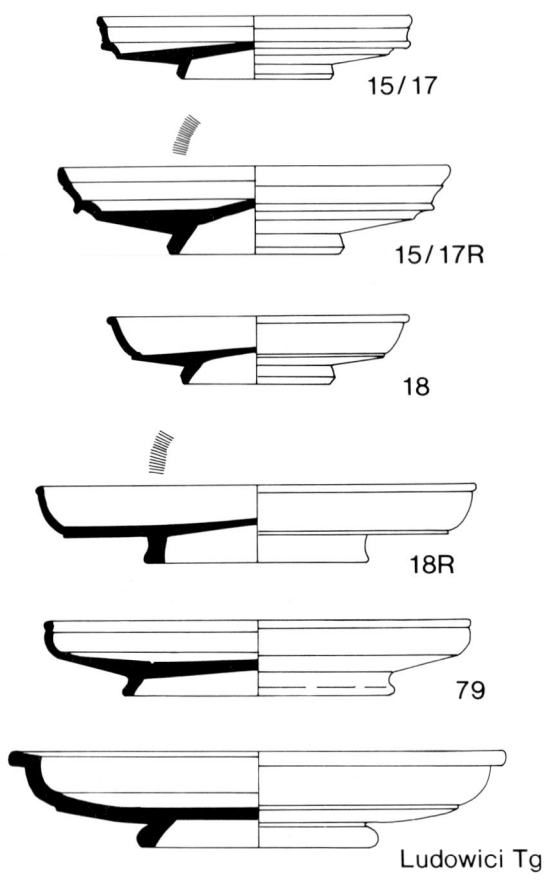

Fig 13 Plates and wide dishes

24

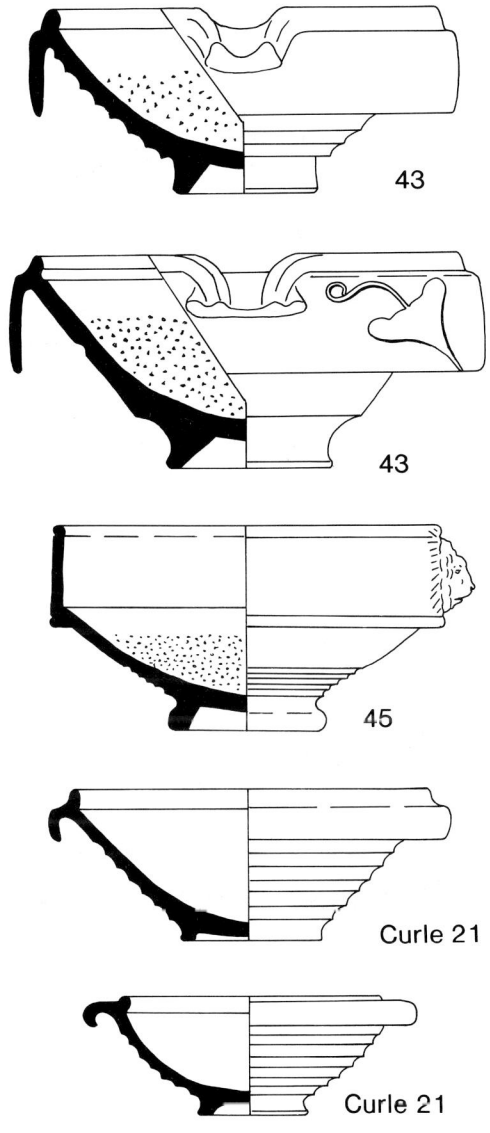

43

43

45

Curle 21

Curle 21

Fig 14 Mortaria and mortar-like bowls

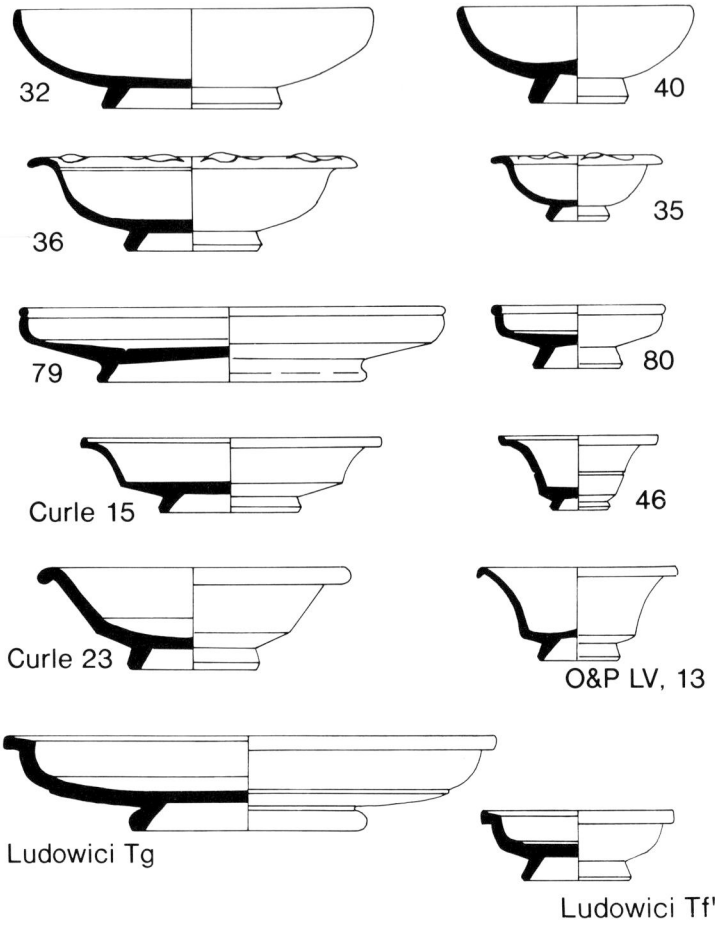

32

40

36

35

79

80

Curle 15

46

Curle 23

O&P LV, 13

Ludowici Tg

Ludowici Tf'

Fig 15 Sets

26

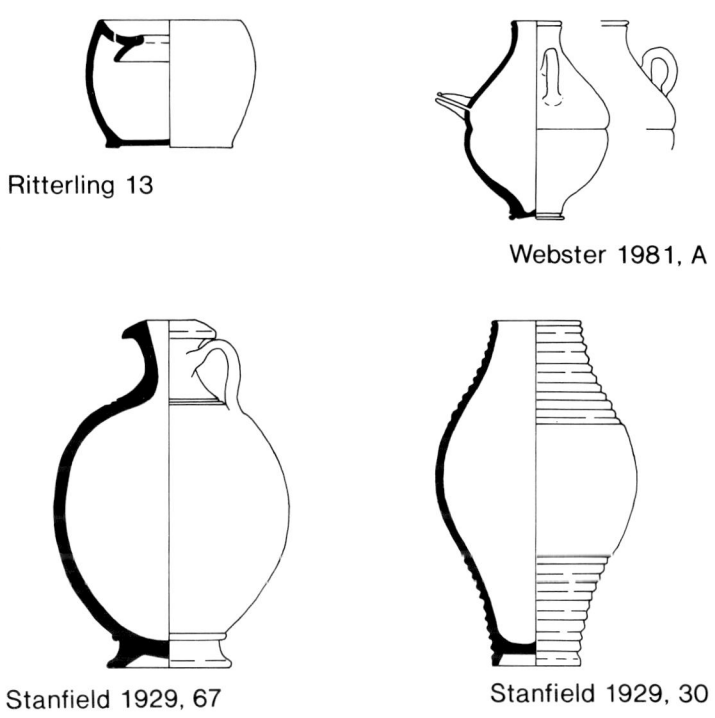

Ritterling 13

Webster 1981, A

Stanfield 1929, 67

Stanfield 1929, 30

Fig 16 Some undecorated closed vessels

Catalogue

The vessels below are catalogued in numerical order, starting with the Dragendorff-Déchelette-Knorr-Walters series, and moving on to vessels from the classifications of Curle, Ludowici, Oswald & Pryce, and Ritterling. Mould-decorated forms are considered in general terms only. Their decoration will be considered in a later section.

Where several forms belong together, either in a single developmental sequence (as in the 18–18/31–31 series) or in a cup/dish set (as with forms 32 and 40), these will be treated together with cross-references within the numerical sequence as appropriate.

R Forms

The letter R after a form number indicates rouletting. This is usually in the form of a circle of rouletting, internally, approximately above the footring. Plain forms may show other differences between their rouletted and unrouletted versions, particularly in the angle of the wall to the base and in the shape of the footring. The R suffix has also been used here to denote forms such as 30 and 37 in which the decoration, normally moulded, has been replaced by rouletting.

Scale

Complete vessels are 1:4. Details are 1:2.

The Dragendorff-Déchelette-Knorr-Walters Series

FORM 11

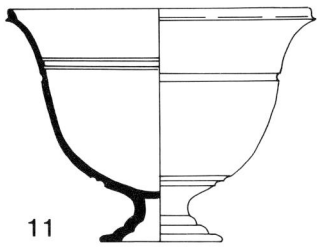

Fig 17

Characteristics

A decorated form. A bell-like bowl with a hollow pedestal foot. A double row of fluting divides a lower zone of decoration from the upper wall, which is largely plain, although it can have rouletted bands upon it. The upper edge of the decorated zone is generally delineated by an ovolo. The rim varies, but always projects beyond the line of the remainder of the vessel.

Dating

The form is Italian in origin and many examples to be seen in British museums will be Arretine and imported in recent times (these include many previously thought to be from London, cf Pryce and Oswald 1928, and Marsh 1979a).

However, some South Gaulish 11s were made and these, along with some in Arretine and in 'provincial Arretine' fabric (ie vessels in a fabric and in forms closely similar to Arretine, but from non-Italian centres), appear on very early sites in Britain (cf Dannell in Cunliffe 1971, and Niblett 1985). Most examples on Romano-British sites will be Claudian.

Bibliography

O&P, pp 65–6, pls II, IX, XXI, along with works cited above. For Arretine versions see Kendrick in Ettlinger *et al* 1990, 165–81.

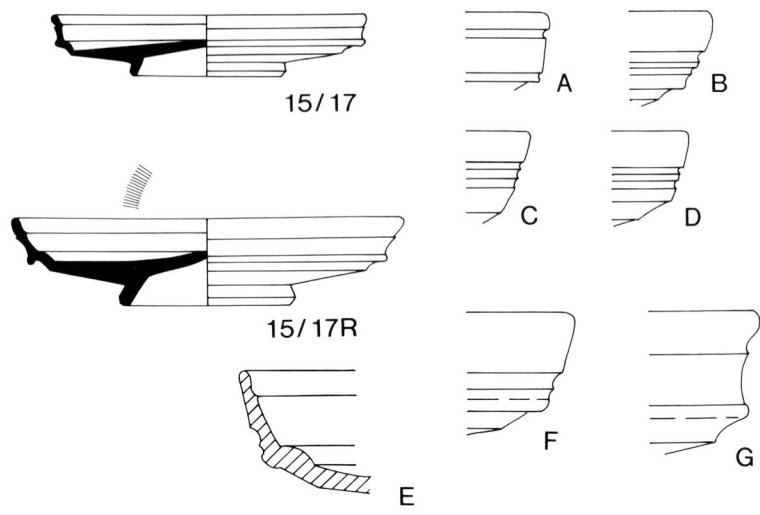

15/17

15/17R

A

B

C

D

E

F

G

Fig 18

Characteristics
A platter with quarter-round moulding internally at the junction of the wall
and the floor. The R Form tends to be deeper with more flared walls. There is
a ridge internally just below the rim. The mouldings on the exterior wall differ
considerably from example to example. A range is shown above (A–G).

Dating
Both 15/17 and 15/17R occurred throughout the 1st century, but declined in
popularity in the Flavian period, when 18 became the most popular plate
form. Occasionally these forms were made at Les Martres-de-Veyre under
Trajan, but the Les Martres form generally had higher walls and some
resemblance to 15/31 (see below).

Bibliography
O&P, pls XLII–XLIII, pp 173–80. A further range of outer wall mouldings is
illustrated by Hawkes and Hull (1947, 181–3, fig 42).

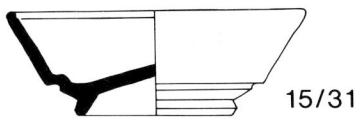

Fig 19

Characteristics
A hybrid form, combining the straight sides and quarter-round moulding of form 15 with the bowl (and often the basal 'kick') of form 31. Form 15/31R also occurs.

Dating
This variant poses some difficulties. Where it shares some of the characteristics of form 31 (as in our illustration) a mid-Antonine date may be suggested (*c* AD 150–175). However, some late versions of form 15/17 produced at Les Martres-de-Veyre can look very similar (although most should have grooved or fluted outer walls) and are presumably early 2nd century.

Bibliography
O&P, pl XLIII, no 43; p 175. The form appears among Lezoux products in Bémont & Jacob (1986, 140, but labelled 'Drag.18/31?'). Terrisse does not illustrate 15/31, but does illustrate another variant which one could term 15/18 (1968, 72, bottom right).

THE 18 TO 31 RANGE

For some reason, presumably connected to usage, this range of forms shows a gradual transition through time, from a plate in the 1st century to a bowl in the mid 2nd century. The change of style was gradual, and the division between 18 and 18/31 and between 18/31 and 31 tends, therefore, to be somewhat arbitrary. As a rough 'rule of thumb', most 18/31s have a ratio of height to width of between 1:4.25 and 1:3.5. R Forms are distinguished by the presence of a ring of rouletting in the basal interior and generally by a squarer footring and greater size.

FORMS 18 and 18R

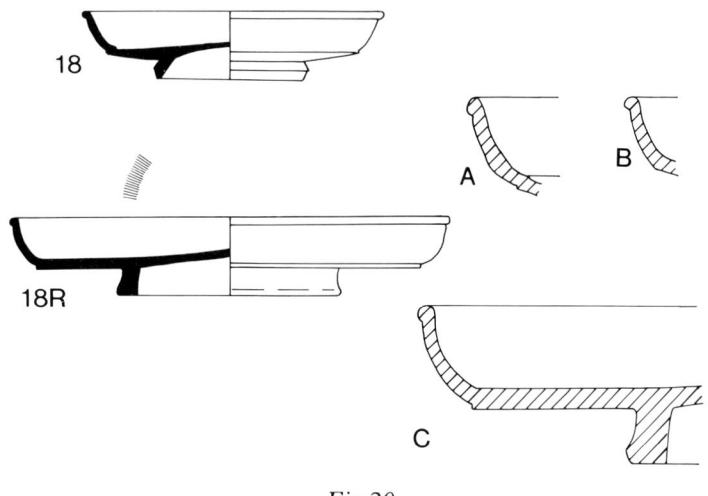

Fig 20

Characteristics
A plate with curved wall and beaded lip. There is often a slight offset or 'step' externally at the junction of the wall and the floor in early examples (see detail A) and a slight internal ridge is also possible. The floor rises slightly in the centre. 18R tends to have a square footring and often a stronger external offset (C). The wall can be higher than in 18.

Dating and Bibliography
See below.

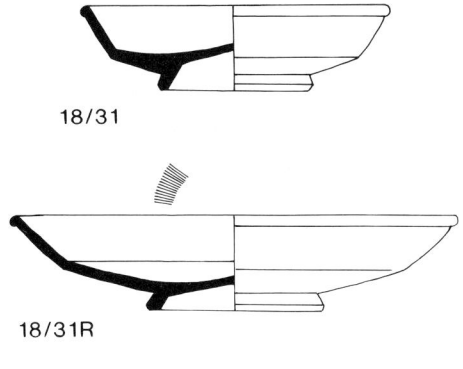

18/31

18/31R

Fig 21

Characteristics

The form is transitional between a plate and a bowl. In 18/31 the angle between the wall and the floor is shallower than in 18 but still present. The floor rises in the centre but less markedly than in 31 and 31R. In 18/31R the division between wall and floor is vestigial but still represented by a slight angle (cf 31 below). The footrings share the characteristics of 18 and 18R forms.

Dating and Bibliography
See below.

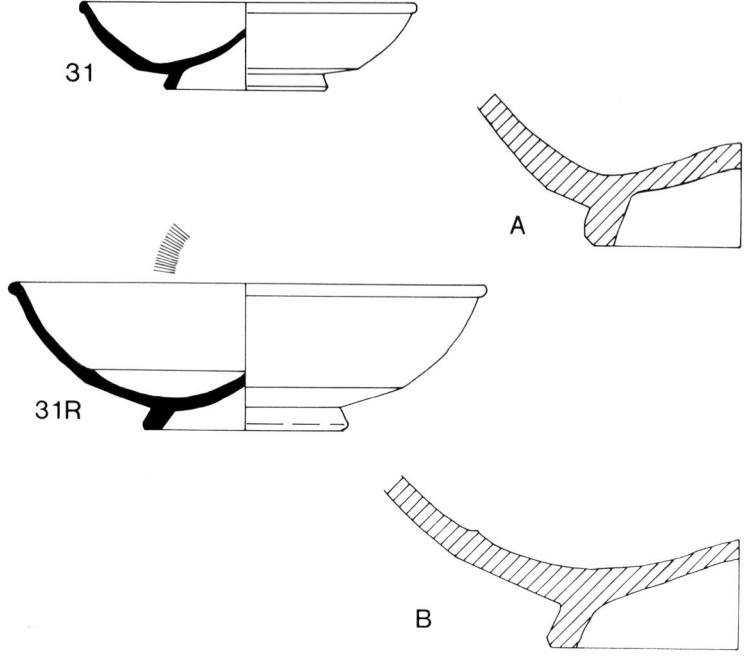

Fig 22

Characteristics

A bowl. In form 31 the division between wall and floor is still apparent externally and the floor frequently begins rising internally at about this point to give the typical convex basal interior (see detail A). The wall and floor of form 31R form a continuous curve with the junction of the two marked by a slight ledge or ridge internally (detail B) and a slight angle externally. The floor generally rises more markedly in 31 than in 31R. Later East Gaulish versions of 31R do not always have the rouletted circle on the floor and the internal junction of base and wall is often marked by a groove.

The hybrid form 15/31 may also be noted (see above).

Dating and Bibliography
See below.

The 18 to 31 range: dating

Forms 18 and 18R
In British contexts, these are mid to mid/late 1st century. The transition to 18/31 and 18/31R is gradual. By mid-Flavian times, many but not all 18s and 18Rs were noticeably less plate-like (ie not so wide), and vessels which can be ascribed to the transitional dish/bowl form 18/31 and 18/31R had probably emerged by the late Flavian period.

Forms 18/31 and 18/31R
South Gaulish examples are late Flavian or early Trajanic (approximately AD 90–110), Les Martres examples mainly *c* AD 100–120 and other Central Gaulish examples Hadrianic to early Antonine (*c* AD 120–150).

Forms 31 and 31R
Both forms appeared in the mid 2nd century, but 31R emerged slightly later than 31 and can nearly always be dated later than c AD 160. Both forms were imported from Central Gaul up to the close of exportation from that region (late in the 2nd century). The forms were popular in East Gaul (cf Ludowici forms Sa and Sb, O&P, pl XLVII) and vessels from East Gaulish centres will have been imported into Britain from the late 2nd to the mid 3rd century.

The 18 to 31 range: bibliography
O&P, pls XLV–XLVII, pp 181–4; Hartley 1972, p 29, note 92; Bird 1986, 175–6 shows a range of later vessels.

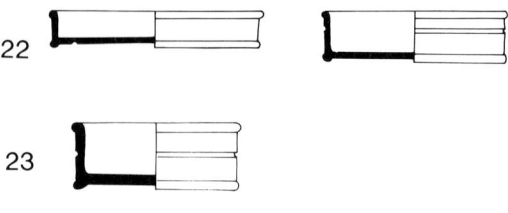

Fig 23

Characteristics
Both small dishes are approximately cylindrical with a slightly recessed base. The rim is usually beaded, and there is generally a similar bead at the base of the wall, acting as a footring. There is often a groove half way up the external wall.

Neither Dragendorff nor Oswald and Pryce are explicit on the criteria, other than size, useful for distinguishing 22 and 23 and it may be that we should really regard both as variations on a single 22/23 theme. Here, however, 22 is regarded as wider and comparatively shallower than 23.

Dating
First century. Both can be present from the conquest in Britain, but are characteristically Flavian.

Bibliography
O&P, pl L, pp 188–9.

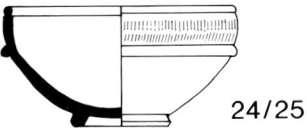

24/25

Fig 24

Characteristics
A hemispherical cup with an external cordon. The rim is beaded or has external and internal grooves immediately below the lip. A rouletted zone lies between the cordon and the rim.

Dating
The form was made at both La Graufesenque and Lezoux in the 1st century and La Graufesenque production certainly continued in the Flavian period. However, most examples found in Britain are pre-Flavian.

Bibliography
O&P, pl XL, pp 171–2.

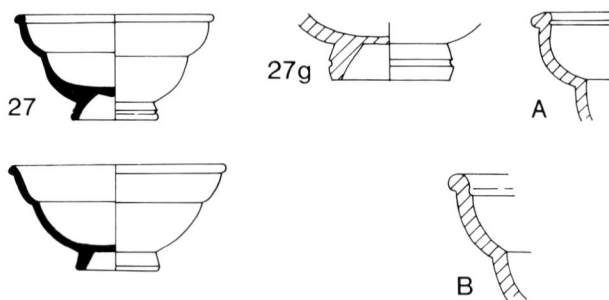

Fig 25

Characteristics

A cup with a double curved wall and a beaded rim. There is an internal groove or offset just below the rim. An external groove on the footring may occur on 1st century examples (distinguished as *form 27g*; cf Hartley in Frere 1972, 216).

Dating

First century examples tend to have strong curves and the earliest examples have flat-topped rims (see detail A). A strong internal groove and the grooved footring are also 1st century features. Flatter profiles (as in the lower of the two complete vessels illustrated and detail B) occur in the 2nd century. The form went out of production *c* AD 150–160, except perhaps in a few East Gaulish factories.

Bibliography

O&P, pl XLIX, pp 186–8; Hartley 1972, pp 29–30.

FORM 29

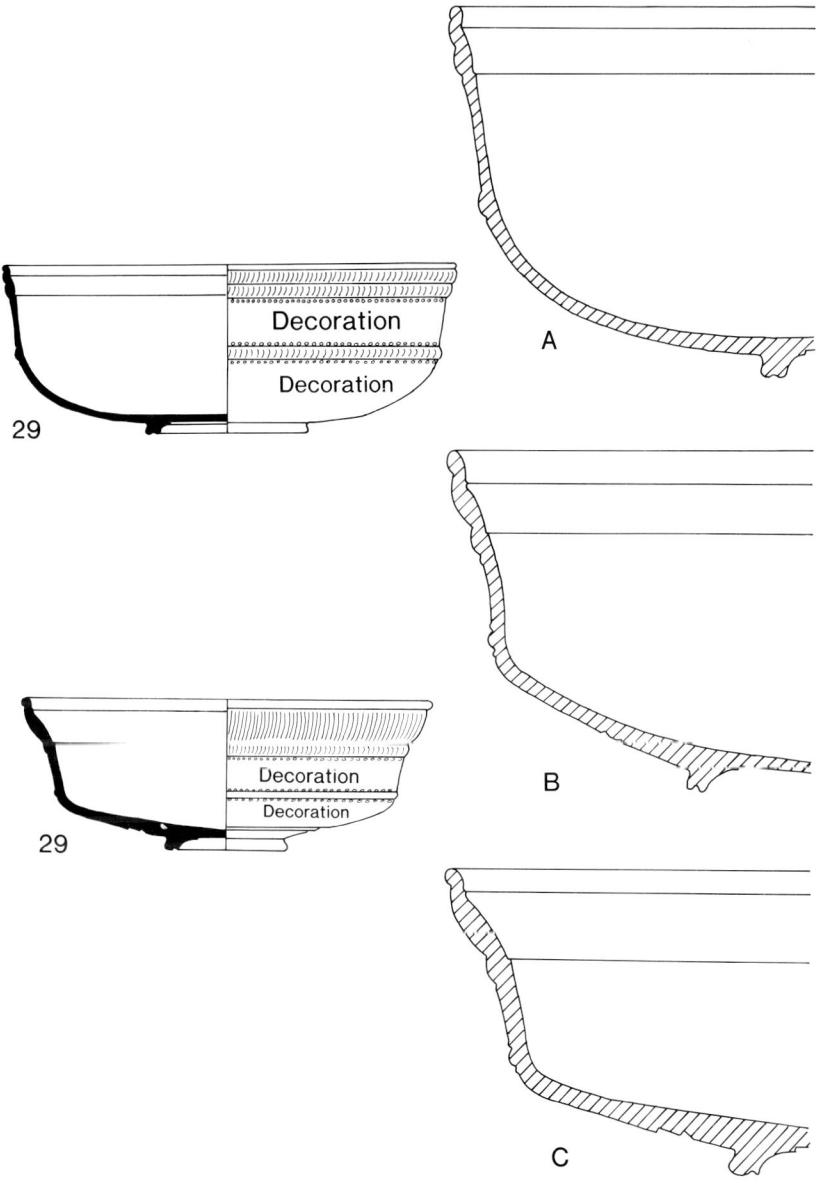

Fig 26

FORM 29 (see Fig 26)

Characteristics

A decorated form, this is generally described as a carinated bowl, although the carination is more obvious in later (eg early/mid Flavian) examples, such as the lower of the two complete vessels illustrated (and details B–C) than in earlier (eg Tiberian/Claudian) examples, such as the upper complete vessel (and detail A).

The upper exterior is rouletted above two zones of decoration divided by a cordon near the point where the wall changes direction. In earlier (Tiberian and very early Claudian) examples the cordon can also be rouletted. On most examples seen in Britain the under-surface of the footring is grooved with an adjacent quarter-round moulding (see details B–C). The cordon is generally bounded on either side by bead rows.

The rim is beaded. Details A–C show how, internally, there is a slight ledge at about the same point as the top of the decoration externally. Above this ledge, the interior shows a double curve. The details indicate how the portion above the moulded decoration becomes larger and more splayed across time.

The rouletted upper rim and the distinctive base, with groove and quarter-round moulding within the footring, frequently become detached from the decoration, and may not immediately appear to belong to a decorated form if found as sherds.

Dating

It is the decoration which will give the greatest precision in dating and this is considered separately (p 74ff below). Here, however, we may note that the form appeared in the Tiberian period and was already popular by the time of the Claudian conquest. The earliest vessels are almost hemispherical and usually have trailing plant designs. Later vessels are more sharply carinated (detail B: Neronian–early Flavian; detail C: early/mid Flavian). Mid-century designs tend to be largely inanimate and winding plant designs again predominate. Flavian vessels make more use of panel decoration and increasing use of animal figures.

The form went out of general production c AD 85 in South Gaul, although it was made *very* occasionally in Central Gaul up to the Hadrianic period (cf Stanfield & Simpson 1958 or 1990, pls 27, 39, 44, & 167).

Polak suggests (1993) that the groove on the footring moved from near the outside on early examples to near the inside on Flavian pieces, and that this was accompanied by a gradual extension of the curve of the quarter-round moulding. This progression can be seen on details B and C, which are in chronological order. It should again be emphasised, however, that considerations of form are secondary to those of decoration when considering the date of 29s.

Bibliography
O&P, pls III–VI. O&P, pp 66–86 discusses both form and decoration. Polak 1993 proposes a classification of footring forms. For a discussion of decoration see p 74ff below.

FORM 30

Characteristics

An approximately cylindrical bowl. Like form 37, the rim is beaded and the upper part of the exterior plain. The decorated zone is bounded at the top by an ovolo (egg-and-tongue) border. The main decorative designs make use of about two thirds of the external vertical surface. Below the decorated zone is an offset over a curved basal section.

The footring is often pad-like (detail E), but can be more elaborate than that on form 37 (eg detail D). Internally, there is a groove or grooves (details

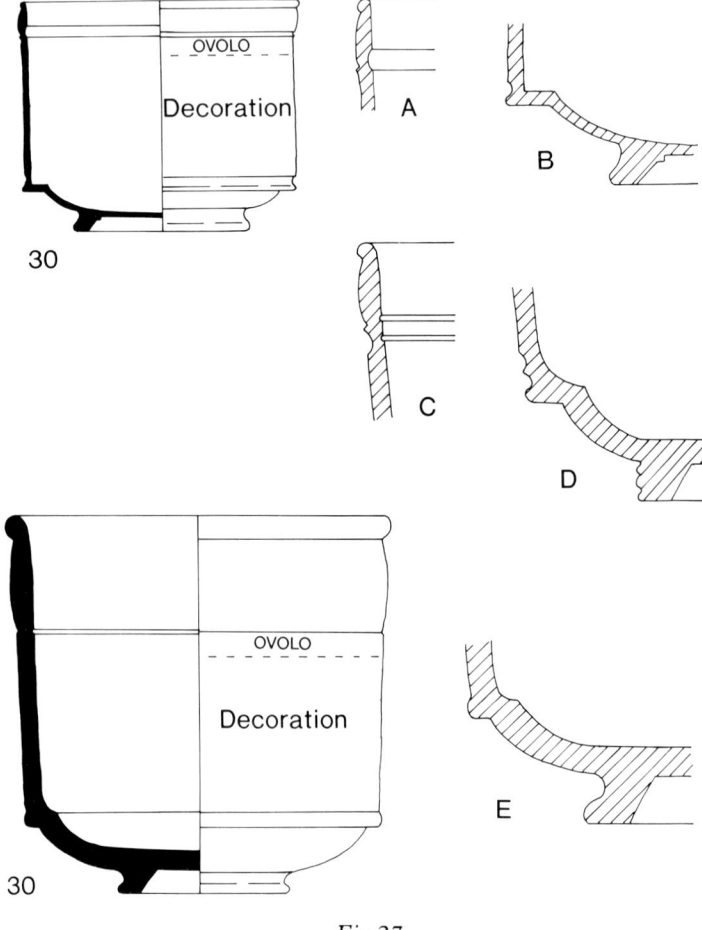

Fig 27

A and C) approximately level with the top of the external decoration. The plain beaded upper rim and the plain basal section can become detached from the moulded decoration, and may not immediately suggest a decorated form if found as sherds.

Dating
The type was made throughout the exporting period and East Gaulish examples were imported into Britain in small numbers into the 3rd century. Multiple internal grooves or an internal broad single flute are characteristic of the 1st century. A small single internal groove is typical of the 2nd century. Mid and mid/late 1st century examples often have a markedly shorter rim than later examples (compare details A/C with the lower complete vessel), and can have mouldings above the decoration (detail C). Decorative styles tend to reflect those of the more popular 29s and 37s (see p 77ff) although always with a tendency to treat the zone available for decoration as a single unit rather than adapt the two-zoned form 29 designs. There is also sometimes a certain archaic tendency on South Gaulish 30s, so that designs which would be pre-Flavian on form 29 can be Flavian on form 30. As with form 29, it should be emphasised that decoration is a more precise guide to dating than is form.

Rouletted Variants

Fig 28

Rouletted variants, termed here 30R occur mainly in the 2nd century. They tend to be smaller, narrower and slightly more conical than true 30s, and are often in a markedly redder fabric.

Bibliography
O&P, pls VII–X, pp 86–95 for both form and decoration. For 30R see pls LXXV, LXXVI and p 22. For decoration see below p 77ff.

FORM 31
See Forms 18–31, p 32 above.

FORMS 32 and 40

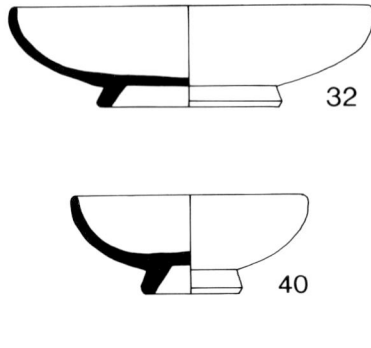

Fig 29

Characteristics
A cup and dish 'set' with plain curving sides and a footring. The forms are mainly East Gaulish in manufacture. Examples of form 32 from earlier East Gaulish factories (such as Blickweiler and La Madeleine) tend to rise slightly at the centre of the floor.

Dating
Predominantly late 2nd century. East Gaulish examples may have been imported up to the mid 3rd century.

Bibliography
Form 32: O&P, pl LXIII, pp 205–6.
Form 40: O&P, pl XLVIII, nos 10–16; pp 185–6.

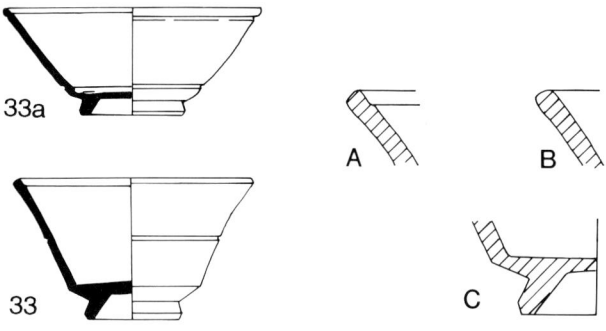

Fig 30

Characteristics

A conical cup with a footstand. Often there is an offset just below the rim internally (detail A), and a groove or grooves on the wall externally. Vessels with an internal moulding at the junction of the wall and base (as in the upper complete vessel) have been termed *form 33a*. The internal floor is often flat (detail C) or slightly convex. The base is chamfered (detail C).

Dating

The type appeared under Tiberius. In Britain it was never common in the 1st century, when form 27 was the most popular cup. Form 33a was made in the 1st century and in the 2nd up to Hadrianic times. Form 33 became the most popular cup form in the mid and late 2nd century.

First century examples tend to have straight or slightly convex walls, and generally have grooves at the top and bottom of the external wall (as in the upper complete vessel). Second century examples tend to have slightly concave walls and a single groove half way down the wall externally (as in the lower complete vessel).

East Gaulish 33s were made into the 3rd century. Later Trier and Rheinzabern vessels are generally without potters' stamps.

Bibliography

O&P, pl LI, pp 189–191; Hartley 1969, p 246; Hartley 1972, p 3, note 6.

45

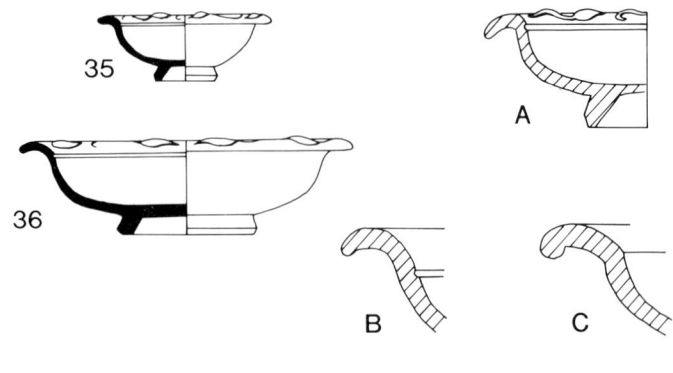

Fig 31

Characteristics
A cup (35) and dish (36) with curved walls and overhanging rim. There is usually a groove internally at the junction of wall and rim (details A and B). Trailed leaves were normally applied to the rim. The forms rarely have potters' stamps except sometimes in the case of East Gaulish products. Later East Gaulish versions of form 36 often have heavy rims with a marked bead below (detail C). Forms 35 and 36 probably formed a cup, dish and bowl set with Form Curle 11.

Dating
Vernhet (1976, 15) suggests that the forms were developed in the 60s AD but are predominantly Flavian or later. This is borne out by the Usk sample (Tyers in Manning 1993, 136). Form 36 is more common in the late 2nd century than earlier.

Bibliography
O&P, pl LIII, pp 192–4; see also Vernhet in Bémont and Jacob 1986, p 99 with references.

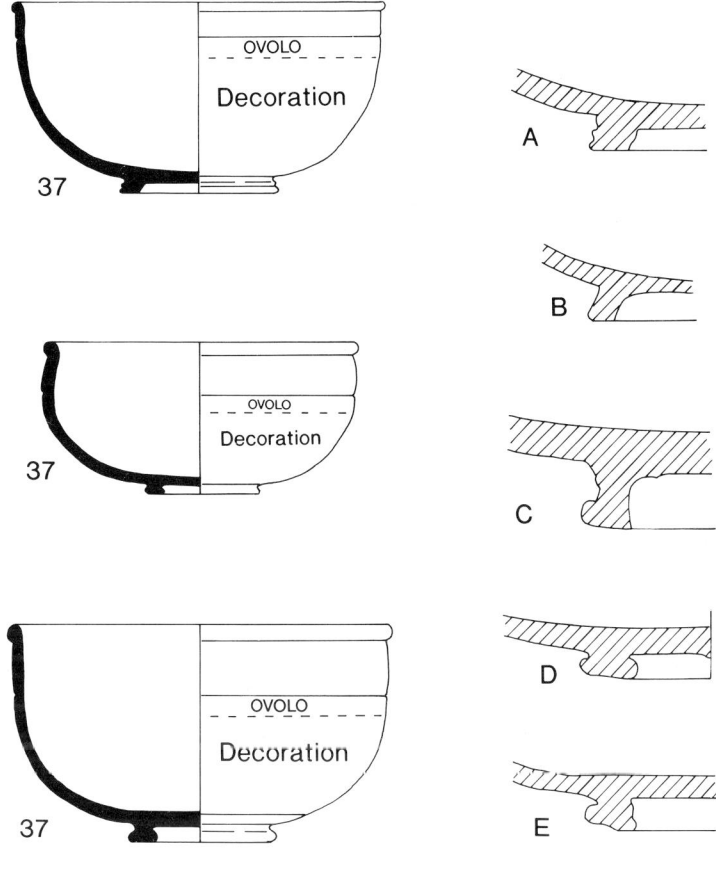

Fig 32

Characteristics

A hemispherical decorated bowl. The upper exterior is plain with a beaded rim. The decorated zone is bounded at the top by a band of ovolo (egg-and-tongue). The footring is pad-like and can show evidence of having been added after moulding (a range of footrings are shown in details A–E). The interior is plain.

Dating

The overall date range is *c* AD 70 to the end of samian exportation (ie to the late 2nd century in the case of Central Gaulish vessels, and the mid 3rd in the case of some East Gaulish). The type emerged *c* AD 70, and became the most popular decorated bowl by the early 80s at the latest. Typological development is slight. However, earlier 37s (such as the upper complete vessel which is Flavian) have a much shorter plain zone above the decoration than most 2nd century examples (eg our lower two complete vessels). Later East Gaulish vessels can have a plain zone above the decoration which is very large indeed. The footring has often been formed by adding a pad-like ring of clay. However, some South Gaulish footrings have clearly been formed by turning. The plain zone above the decoration and the base can become detached from the decoration and may not immediately suggest a decorated vessel if found in sherd form.

As with forms 29 and 30, precision in dating is largely reliant upon analysis of the decoration. This will be discussed later (p 78ff). Here it may be noted that the earliest 37s tend to follow the two-zoned decoration, created with the aid of generally small poinçons, which is characteristic of form 29. Larger panels with figures are typical of later South Gaulish production. Les Martres-de-Veyre tended to produce designs which are finely detailed but tightly packed (and mainly *c* AD 100–120). Larger, more open designs are typically Antonine. East Gaulish designs were frequently achieved with a relatively small number of poinçons.

Rouletted variants
Rouletted variants, termed here *Form 37R*, occasionally occur (Fig 33). They are characteristically Central Gaulish, but were also made in East Gaul (particularly at Heiligenberg). They tend to be smaller than true 37s and are often in a markedly redder fabric than most Central Gaulish ware. Their slip can be abnormal and have a rather East Gaulish 'look' to it. All examples are probably 2nd century.

Bibliography
O&P, pls XI–XVIII, pp 95–125. For rouletted variants see O&P, pl LXXV, pp 221–3.

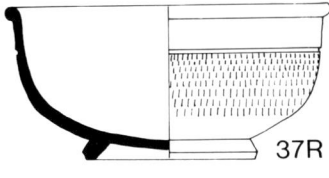

37R

Fig 33

This is most probably part of a single developmental sequence with Ritterling 12 and Curle 11. All will be treated together here.

The Ritterling 12, Curle 11, Dragendorff 38 sequence

FORM RITTERLING 12

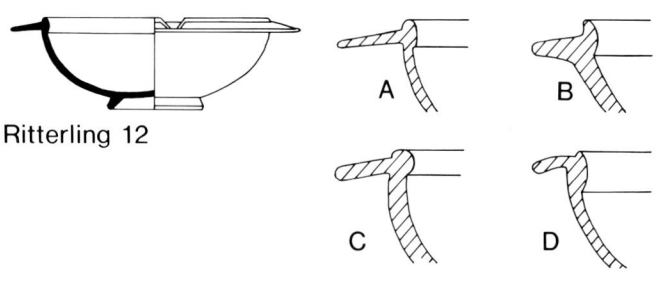

Ritterling 12

Fig 34

Characteristics
A hemispherical bowl with an undecorated straight or slightly curved flange set a short way below the rim (see details A–D). The rim can be interrupted by a small 'spout' which is delineated by two ridges of clay on the flange (as in the complete drawing). The interior of the rim forms a rounded moulding which has the effect of thickening the rim in comparison with the rest of the wall.

Dating
Predominantly pre-Flavian, although there are some early Flavian examples. Production after *c* AD 80 seems improbable.

Bibliography
O&P, pl LXXI, pp 210–11.

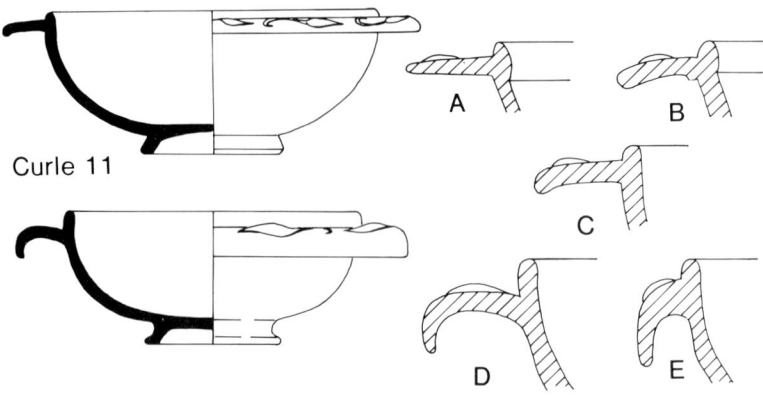

Curle 11

Fig 35

Characteristics
A hemispherical bowl with a flange which is generally a short way below the rim. The flange is decorated with trailed leaves (as on forms 35 and 36, with which Curle 11 probably formed a 'set'). Earlier examples have the internal moulding at the rim of Ritterling 12 (cf details A–B) and their flanges can be straight as also in Ritterling 12 (cf detail A). As time went by, the flange became more hooked and tended to move down the wall of the bowl (details D–E). However, some Les Martres examples of the type have straight chunky flanges with a groove near the edge.

Dating
Curle 11 developed in the Flavian period. Examples sharing characteristics with Ritterling 12 (the flange and moulding as noted above) will be early in the history of the form. Later, flanges became more hooked. Thus detail A would be from an early Flavian bowl, and details B–C from Flavian ones. A markedly curved and prominent flange (as in the lower complete example and details D–E) is a feature of later (usually 2nd century) vessels. Curle 11 was made only as late as the AD 140s.

Bibliography
O&P, pl LXXI, pp 211–12.

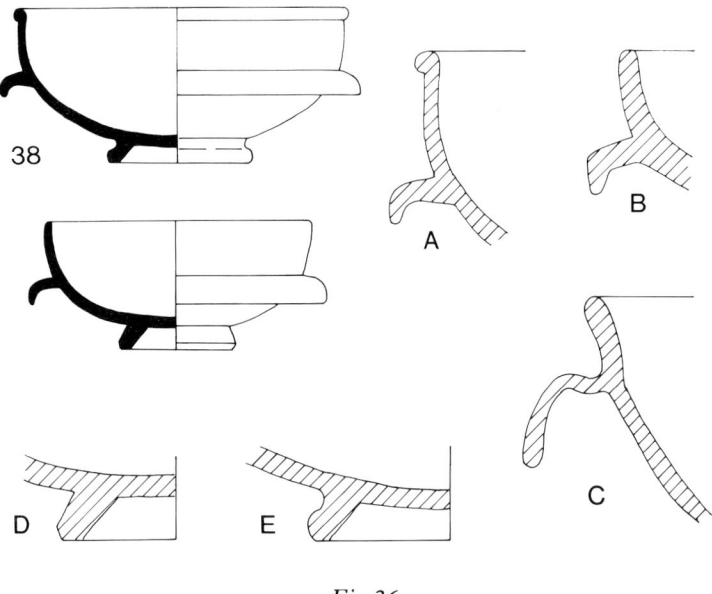

Fig 36

Characteristics

A hemispherical bowl with a plain hooked flange well down the wall. The rim can be beaded or plain. The flange can be curved or angular. Footrings can be chamfered or rounded. The two illustrated vessels and details A–E attempt to encompass most variations. It may be noted, however, that form 44 and even form 81, can be regarded as variants of 38.

Dating

The type emerged in the late Hadrianic period but is typical of the second half of the 2nd century. East Gaulish examples continued to be imported up to the mid 3rd century. Variations in rim and footring are illustrated.

The type also appears frequently, and with variations, in later, non-samian, red slip fabrics (eg Oxfordshire red colour-coated ware).

Bibliography

O&P, pl LXXII, pp 212–14.

FORM 40
See Form 32 above

FORM 42

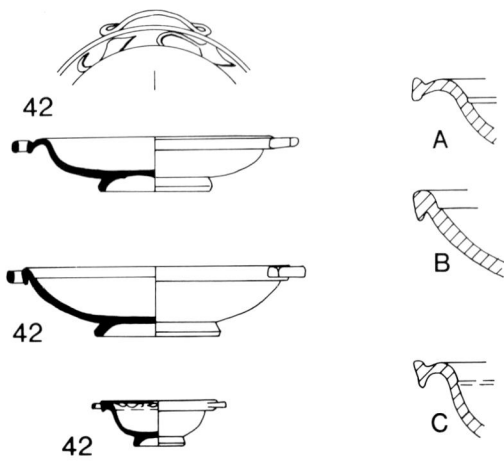

Fig 37

Characteristics
A dish or cup with applied strap handles at the rim. There is a curved wall and a footstand. A variety of dishes (and even a related cup) are grouped under this form number, the uniting feature being the occurrence of applied strap handles, although these will not, of course, appear on all sherds. Rims either curl over (detail B) or end in a short wall like the letter 'T' on its side (as in detail A). A typical plan view of a strap handle is illustrated. Rims may have the trailed leaf decoration of our upper and lower examples.

Dating
Flavian to Hadrianic. It is, however, more characteristic of Central than of South Gaul.

Bibliography
O&P, pl LIV, pp 194–5.

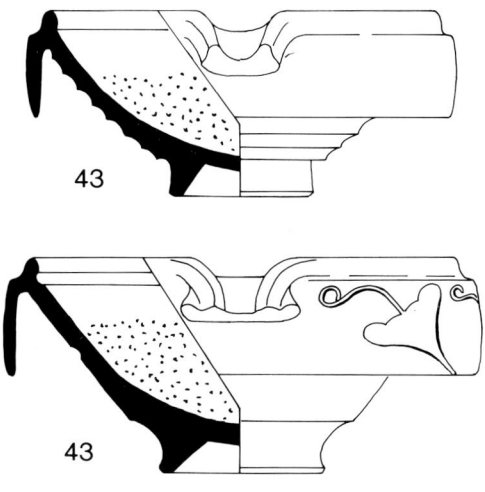

Fig 38

Characteristics

A mortarium with similarities to Curle 21 (qv) but with the trituration grits of a true mortarium. The overhanging flange is deeper than in Curle 21, and can be decorated *en barbotine*.

Dating

Predominantly late 2nd century (post *c* AD 170) and later. Most examples are East Gaulish, and so importation up to the mid 3rd century is possible.

Bibliography

O&P, pl LXXIII, p 215.

FORM 44

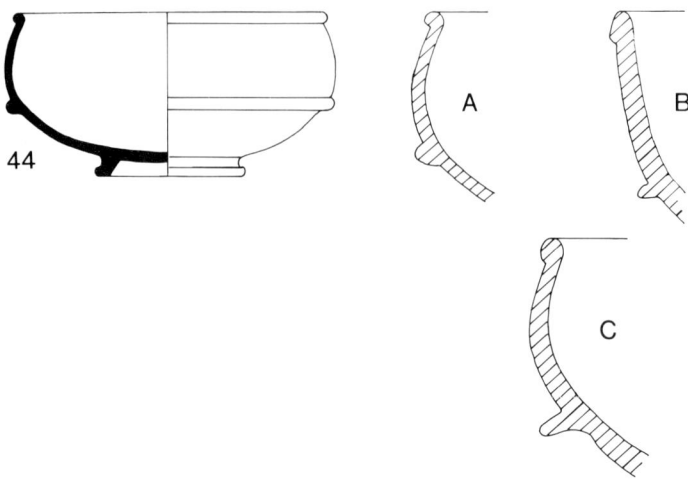

Fig 39

Characteristics
A bowl resembling form 38 but with a cordon instead of a flange. The bowl tends to be more globular than 38. The rim is beaded. There is also a similarity with some examples of form 81 (qv), and it is possible that 44 and 81 should both be regarded as variants of form 38.

East Gaulish centres, at Trier and Rheinzabern in particular, produced a number of variants with barbotine or rouletted decoration; cf O&P, pl LXII (barbotine) and pl LXXVI, 5 (rouletting).

Dating
As form 38, ie the form emerged by the late Hadrianic period but was most popular in the second half of the 2nd century. East Gaulish vessels may have been imported up to the mid 3rd century.

Bibliography
O&P, pl LXI, nos 1–6, pp 203–4; for the variants with barbotine decoration, Ludowici SMb and SMc, O&P, pl LXII, pp 204–5; for a variant with rouletting, O&P, pl LXXVI, no 5, p 222.

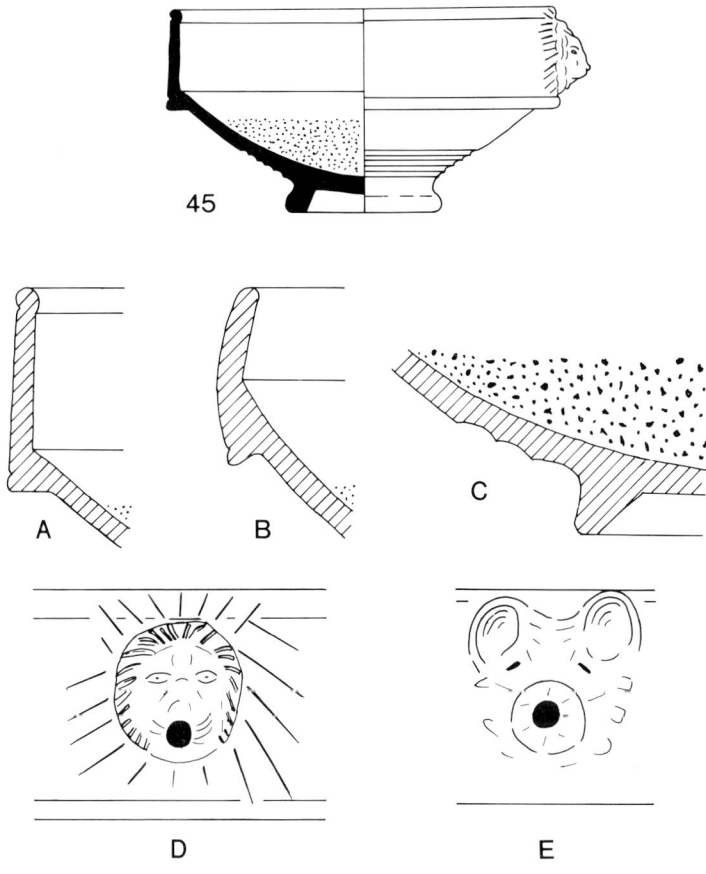

Fig 40

Characteristics

A samian mortarium with a near upright wall. There is an offset or overhang at the junction of the upper and lower walls. A spout, generally in the form of a moulded, open-mouthed lion, was applied to the outside of the upper wall. It is often surrounded by incised and radiating lines as in detail D. The lion-head can appear in degenerate form, in which case it looks very bat-like (compare details D and E). The upper wall is often bounded by grooves top and bottom (detail A). Examples with curved upper walls (detail B) can occur. The trituration grits, which give the mortarium its internal grinding surface, usually occupy only the lower part of the vessel, so that upper wall fragments may not immediately appear to belong to a mortarium. As with other samian mortaria, the grit has been applied before slipping and appears coated in slip on unused vessels.

Note: for other mortaria see forms 43 and Curle 21.

Dating
The type first appears in the late 2nd century (*c* AD 170 or later). East Gaulish examples were imported up to the mid 3rd century.

Bibliography
O&P, pl LXXIV, pp 216–17; Bird 1986, pp 178–85 shows a range of spouts.

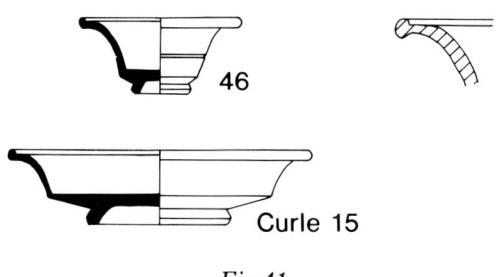

Fig 41

Characteristics

These make up a cup (46) and dish (Curle 15) 'set'. Both forms have flaring walls which are concave externally. The rims generally turn upwards at the top of the external concavity (see detail). Variations, particularly of the rim, may occur (cf O&P, pls LVLVI). The internal base is not always flat but can be slightly concave. The forms are presumably related to the forms Curle 23, O&P, LV, 13, (classified with form 46 by O&P but treated here as the cup version of Curle 23) and form 42 (qv).

Dating

These forms appear from the late 1st century and continue throughout the importing period, but they are predominantly 2nd century and most common in the pre-Antonine period. For later, East Gaulish, versions of 46 which may have been imported up to the mid 3rd century, see O&P, pl LV, nos 19–25.

Bibliography

O&P, pls LV–LVI, pp 195–198. Also Vernhet in Bémont & Jacob 1986, p 99 for 'sets'.

FORM 54

This and other beakers are treated with Form 72.

FORM 64

Fig 42

Characteristics

A conical decorated beaker. The rim is beaded. There is a plain band below the rim externally. The decoration is bounded above and below by one or more grooves or cordons. There is a plain band below. The footstand is splayed. The form can appear in a very orange fabric or with a black gloss.

Dating

The form was made by a few Central Gaulish potters in the first half of the 2nd century. Bémont has made a study of the decorative details, many of which appear to be particular to the form.

Bibliography

O&P, pl XXI, nos 4–6, p 127 for the form. Bémont 1977 for decorative details.

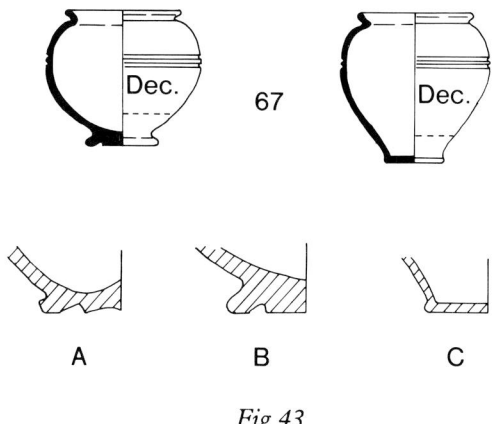

Fig 43

Characteristics
A small globular mould-decorated beaker. The rim is everted and the upper part of the vessel plain (otherwise a two-part mould would have been required to produce the decoration and samian potters rarely used these). The decoration, often without an ovolo border, is bounded above by two or more grooves, generally at about the point of maximum girth. The base is usually solid, but details of both the base and the rim vary considerably (cf O&P, pl XXI and our details A–C). The interior shows the characteristic finger-rilling of 'closed' vessels but 67 was sufficiently wide at the neck to allow slip to enter without an airlock forming so the interior is slipped (unlike some other closed vessels). Occasionally barbotine decoration occurs.

Dating
Flavian and early 2nd century.

Bibliography
O&P, pl XXI, nos 8–13, pp 126–7, 222. There has been no specific study of the decorative schemes, many of which appear to be peculiar to the form, but Hermet 1934, pl 90 shows a range.

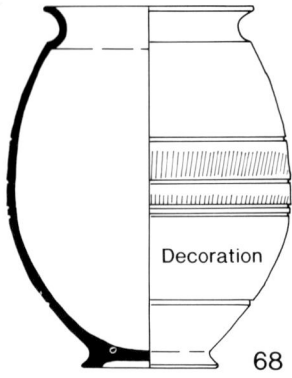

Fig 44

Characteristics
A decorated jar which is considerably larger than form 67 (see above). The decorated zone is on the lower half of the external wall with, below it, a plain band and splayed footstand. Above the decoration, grooves divide bands of rouletting around the girth. The upper exterior is plain. The rim is curved above a clearly defined shoulder. The interior shows the finger-rilling characteristic of 'closed' vessels but, as with 67, the neck is wide enough to allow the interior to be slipped. The form can appear in black slipped ware. Form 68 is markedly less common than smaller but contemporary closed forms such as 72 and its variants.

Dating
A Central Gaulish form. Mid to late 2nd century.

Bibliography
O&P, pl XXI, no 15, p 128.

FORM 72 AND OTHER BEAKERS

Here we have gathered together a number of beakers and small jars which are clearly related. Plain versions can occur, but many are decorated, usually with trailed decoration (*en barbotine*) although sometimes by other means, including incised ('cut-glass') decoration. The most common form (72) will be considered first.

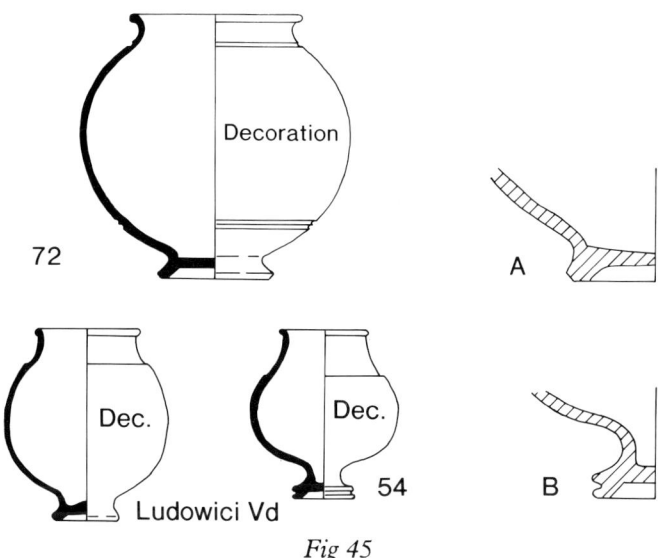

Fig 45

FORM 72

Characteristics

A globular beaker with a decorated zone delineated above and below with grooves. There is a plain band above the footstand, which is splayed. The neck starts almost immediately above the decorated zone and is curved outwards. The rim is generally beaded. The interior shows the finger-rilling characteristic of 'closed' vessels but is also slipped.

A wide zone of moulded decoration running on both sides of the point of maximum girth could not be achieved without the use of a double mould. Although such moulds are not unknown (eg on certain South Gaulish flagons) they were not used for form 72 which, instead, was decorated using incised 'cut-glass' decoration or applied barbotine. Occasionally, undecorated examples occur, cf O&P, pl LXXIX, no 1.

Forms 54 and Ludowici Vd are related beakers (see below).

Dating
Second half of the 2nd century. East Gaulish vessels could have been imported up to the mid 3rd century.

Bibliography
O&P, pl LXXVII, pp 224–6 ('cut-glass' vessels); O&P, pl LXXIX, pp 226–30 (vessels decorated *en barbotine*); O&P, LXXXIV, nos 1–2, pp 230–1 (vessels with applied decoration).

FORM 54 and LUDOWICI FORM Vd

Characteristics
Both are beaker forms with a high neck rising from a shoulder, and with a bead rim. The drawing of Form 54 by Dragendorff is somewhat indefinite, and the form was subdivided by Ludowici as his forms Vd–Vg (plain versions) and VMg (decorated). Form 54, as drawn here, has a pedestal base which is grooved to give a 'pulley-wheel' appearance and is Ludowici form Vg. Ludowici Vd has a similar rim and neck but rises from a wider and simpler base. They are illustrated here as just two examples of a range of beakers allied to form 72. Such vessels can be plain or have barbotine or 'cut-glass' decoration.

Dating
Probably second half of the 2nd century. East Gaulish vessels may have been imported up to the mid 3rd century. Third century forms are discussed by Bird (1993).

Bibliography
O&P, pl LXXVII, nos 5–6, and pl LXXIX, pp 223–31. See also O&P, pls LXXXLXXXI, pp 223–31 for other beakers with 'pulley-wheel' bases and Bird 1993.

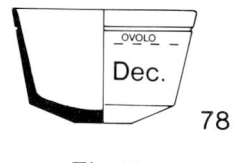

Fig 46

Characteristics
A small carinated bowl with moulded decoration. The rim is plain. The decoration is sometimes bounded by an ovolo above, and resembles that on form 30 to which this form may be related. There is no decoration below the carination and no footstand.

Dating
Predominantly Flavian to Trajanic, with a few 2nd century examples from Central and East Gaul.

Bibliography
O&P, pl XXI, pp 125–6. There have been no separate studies of the decorative schemes on this form, but a range is illustrated by Hermet (1934, pl 92).

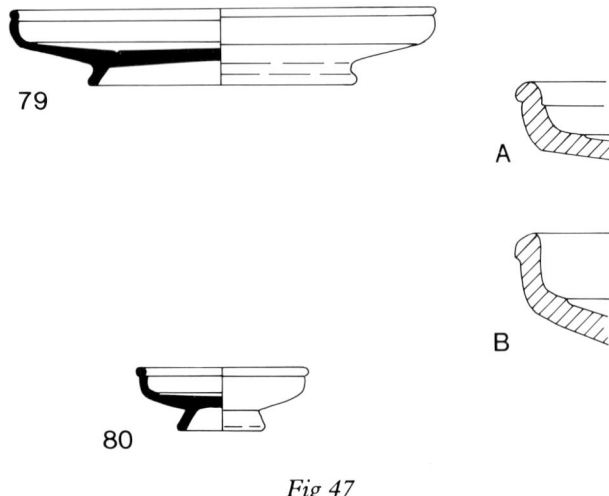

Fig 47

Characteristics
A cup (80) and dish (79) 'set', with strongly curving walls and a beaded rim. There is an internal groove or offset just below the rim. There is also a slight step internally at the junction of wall and floor (see details A–B). Forms 79 and 80 are thicker than forms 27 and 18 with which small fragments might be confused. A version of form 79 with an internal rouletted circle as in the 18R to 31R series was produced, and is termed *form 79R*. East Gaulish versions of form 79 tend to be more bowl-like (cf Ludowici form Th, O&P, pl LVIII, no 4 Bird 1993, Fig 3) merging with bead-rim variants of form 32.

Dating
The forms probably emerged *c* AD 160, although 79R may have appeared later than this. East Gaulish vessels will have been imported into the 3rd century.

Bibliography
O&P, pl LVIII, pp 199–200; Hartley 1972, particularly pp 29–30.

FORM 81

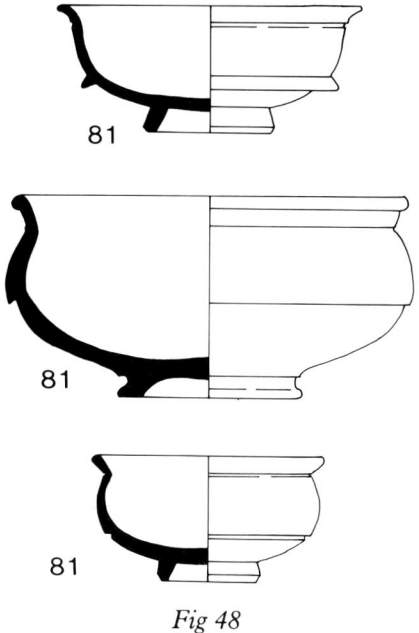

81

81

81

Fig 48

Characteristics

A necked bowl with a wide neck and slightly everted rim. The rim can be plain, curved, or end in a bead. The middle section of the wall thickens, allowing an overhang at a point between a third and a half of the height, as measured from the base upwards.

There are several variants, including one with a double wall (cf O&P, pl LXI) and another with a cordon, as on form 44. We illustrate three versions which, between them, show the main variations.

Potters' stamps may occur on the outer wall.

Dating

Although made in Central Gaul from the Trajanic period, the form was most common in the Hadrianic–Antonine period. East Gaulish examples may have been imported up to the mid 3rd century.

Bibliography

O&P, pl LXI, nos 6–10, pp 203–4. Note that O&P, pl LXI, no 6 is not Ludowici Sn as stated but Ludowici Sk.

Curle Forms

Curle devised his own system of classification for samian from the fort of Newstead (Curle 1911). Most of his forms duplicate those of Dragendorff and are no longer used. However, the following supplement other classifications:

FORM CURLE 11
This is part of a developmental sequence with Ritterling 12 and Form 38 and is considered with form 38 above.

FORM CURLE 15
This forms part of a cup and dish 'set' with form 46 and is considered with it above.

FORM CURLE 21

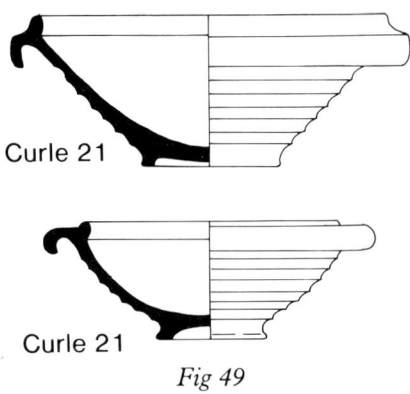

Curle 21

Curle 21

Fig 49

Characteristics
A mortar-like bowl, usually without the trituration grits of a true mortarium, although some Central Gaulish examples (many from Vichy) were gritted. The flange overhangs. Internally, there is a sharp change in wall direction just below the rim. The external wall is fluted horizontally, where visible below the flange. The type is clearly related to the mortarium form 43 (see above).

Dating
Second half of the 2nd century.

Bibliography
O&P, pl LXXIII, nos 1–4, p 214.

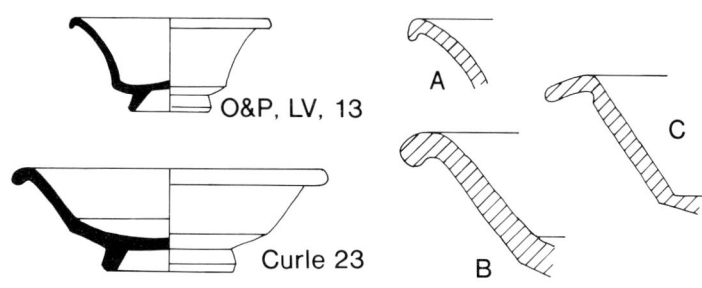

Fig 50

Characteristics

A cup (O&P, LV, 13) and dish (Curle 23) 'set'. The wall curves outwards slightly and ends in a hooked rim (see details A–C). The cup form is classified by O&P under form 46, but is clearly the cup version of Curle 23. Later East Gaulish versions of Curle 23 tend to be more bowl-like.

Dating

The forms were made from the late Flavian period. East Gaulish vessels could have been imported up to the mid 3rd century.

Bibliography

O&P, pl LV, no 13, p 196; see also *ibid* no 19.

Curle 23 with variants: O&P, pl LIX, pp 201–2. See Vernhet in Bémont & Jacob 1986, p 99 with references for 'sets'.

Ludowici Forms

When considering the Rheinzabern site, Ludowici devised a complex classification of forms. A number of these are variants of more common forms, and are considered with them here (eg Ludowici SMb and SMc are mentioned under form 44). The following are, however, sufficiently distinctive and common to deserve separate mention:

LUDOWICI Tg, Tf', and Tx

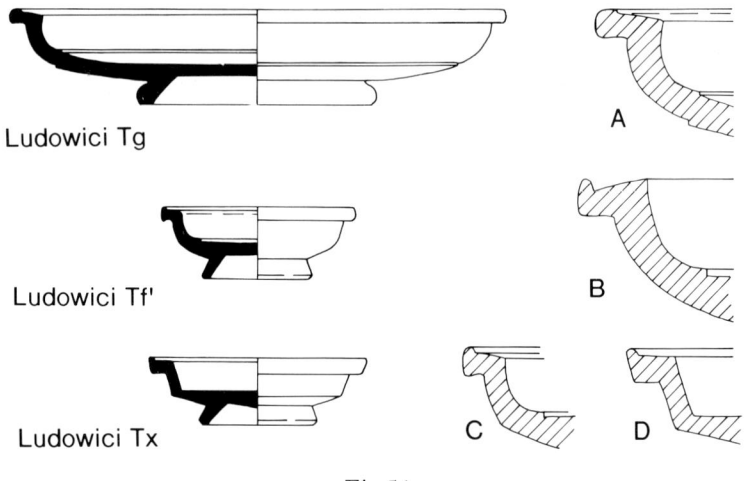

Ludowici Tg

Ludowici Tf'

Ludowici Tx

A

B

C   D

Fig 51

Characteristics
This is another cup (Tf' and Tx) and dish (Tg) 'set'. The lower body of Tg and Tf' resembles forms 79/80 in appearance, but is generally thicker and heavier. The rim is in the form of a flange with an upturn at the edge (details A–C). Ludowici Tg can have a small step at the junction of wall and floor, both externally and internally (detail A), and both cup and dish commonly have the internal step (details B–C).

Ludowici Tx is a more angular and less common version of the cup Tf' (detail D). It is, however, only one version of a range of broadly similar cups (cf O&P, pl LX, nos 2 & 5–8). Recent literature has tended to group these generically under the title Ludowici Tx, but the original classification is preferred here.

Dating
Usually post *c* AD 160. East Gaulish examples may have been imported into the 3rd century.

Bibliography
O&P, pl LX, p 202.

O&P (Oswald and Pryce) Forms

In their major synthesis of samian forms (Oswald and Pryce 1920), the authors were concerned to show significant details and variations within the established classifications. They did not intentionally offer any new classification. However, O&P, pl LV, no 13 is so clearly the cup version of Curle form 23, that it has been separated here and is considered with the Curle form (qv).

Ritterling Forms

Ritterling made his own classification for the samian from the fort at Hofheim. As with other such classifications, a few of his forms not found in Dragendorff are in general use:

FORM RITTERLING 8

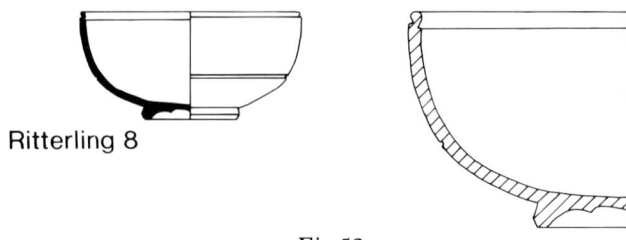

Ritterling 8

Fig 52

Characteristics
A hemispherical cup with an external groove just below the rim and another about half way down the wall. There is an internal offset just below the rim. There is usually fluting inside the footring producing an effect similar to that on a form 29 footring, but smaller and without the footring groove (see detail).

Dating
Pre-Flavian.

Bibliography
O&P, pl XLVIII, nos 4–9, pp 184–5.

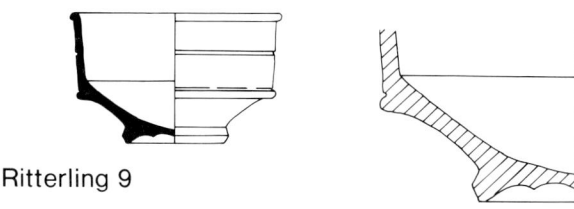

Ritterling 9

Fig 53

Characteristics
A carinated cup with a flattened or bead rim and an external cordon at the point of carination. There is generally an external groove half way up the upper wall. Most examples have fluting inside the footring as on Ritterling 8 (see detail).

Dating
Pre-Flavian. The form is rare after *c* AD 60.

Bibliography
O&P, pl XXXIX, pp 170–1.

FORM RITTERLING 12

This is part of a developmental sequence with form Curle 11 and form 38. It is considered with form 38 above.

FORM RITTERLING 13

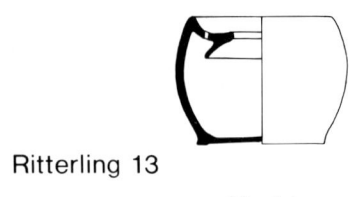

Ritterling 13

Fig 54

Characteristics
An inkwell. The vessel is barrel-shaped, with a circular central opening at the top. There are minor variations in design, particularly of the non-spill aperture (cf O&P, pl LXX). In common with all closed vessels, the interior shows signs of finger-rilling. Due to the shape, air tended to be trapped in the interior when the vessel was dipped in slip, so that slip rarely covers the whole interior (a feature common to many 'closed' vessels with narrow neck openings). To facilitate filling with ink, a hole was often pierced through the top to allow air to escape as ink was poured in. Evidence of ink-staining on the interior is not always found.

Dating
The form was produced throughout the exporting period.

Bibliography
O&P, pl LXX, pp 209–10.

Other plain forms

Although the vast majority of plain ware in any site assemblage will belong to the forms already illustrated, other forms will occasionally occur. The first source of reference for these should be O&P (Oswald & Pryce 1920) where a wide range of forms is included, as well as a large number of variants. It must be borne in mind, however, that Oswald and Pryce were writing over 70 years ago and that their dating, in particular, was only as good as the evidence then available. As a result, some care needs to be taken when using their work.

If an 'oddity' does not occur in O&P, then it is often worth consulting works on specific manufacturing sites, as these can include forms which are rare away from the immediate area of the kilns. Particularly useful here is Bémont & Jacob 1986, which includes ranges from many kiln sites. Gose 1984 (and its earlier editions of 1950, 1975, and 1976) includes a useful range of vessels encountered in the Rhineland (and, therefore, with an East Gaulish bias). Rheinzabern types were classified by Ludowici (cf Ludowici 1908, 271–86; Ludowici 1912, 245–6). Third century East Gaulish forms encountered in Britain are discussed by Bird (1993).

If these sources fail, then a pair of articles on unusual samian forms, written by Stanfield (1929 and 1936), may be of assistance. In addition, there are a few publications which include specific unusual forms, for example the Bignor candlestick (Hartley 1969, 248; Frere 1982, 184) and the so-called 'feeding-bottle' (Webster 1981). Hartley in Frere 1984 also includes a number of unusual forms, including one vessel which appears to confirm the use of templates to produce samian plain forms (it is form 18R externally and form 15 or 15/17 internally). The visual index above (p 27) illustrates three of the more unusual vessels encountered in Britain. They are:

1   The feeding bottle, Webster 1981, A.
2   A flagon, Stanfield 1929, no 67. Stanfield illustrates a number of plain flagons (1929, nos 63, 67–9). O&P also include a number (pls LXXXII–III) although not all of these are in samian ware.
3   One of a series of barrel-like beakers, Stanfield 1929, no 30.

Mention should also be made of two unusual mould-decorated forms, the *lagena* (Stanfield 1929, 114–17 and Stanfield 1937) and the flask or *gourd* (Stanfield 1936, no 16).

However, it is a good general rule always to expect the usual rather than the unusual. If a fragment does not appear to be one of the commonly encountered forms, it is nearly always better to check against the full range of these before considering the rarer types.

5   Decorated forms and their schemes of decoration

Although mould-decorated forms have been mentioned above in the catalogue, more detailed treatment of decoration has been reserved for this chapter. It will be divided into two parts: a) a general consideration of the main decorated forms (29, 30, and 37) with a broad outline of their decorative schemes; b) a guide to the analysis of decoration, which will aim to help in identifying the work of individual potters.

The decoration of forms 29, 30, and 37: a general outline

FORM 29

The form is described on p 40 above. It first appeared in the Tiberian period, but most vessels in Britain will, of course, be post-conquest and thus Claudian or later. The earliest examples are almost hemispherical and usually have trailing plant designs. Later bowls are more sharply carinated. Plant-derived designs continue to predominate on mid-century vessels, but a few small animal figures can also be found here. Flavian designs make more use of panelled decoration and increasing use of animal (and occasionally human) figures. The type went out of production in South Gaul *c* AD 85, although it was made *very* occasionally in Central Gaul up to the Hadrianic period.

Robert Knorr collected a large number of South Gaulish decorative designs associated with makers' stamps. These are published in the two standard works, usually abbreviated as Knorr 1919 and Knorr 1952. When using these, it should be remembered that the names recorded, unless they appear in the decoration, are those of *bowl makers* and that these are not necessarily the same as *mould makers*. Bowl makers may use moulds made by different hands, and so Knorr does not necessarily identify the makers of the moulds for the bowls which he illustrates (see Haalebos, Mees & Polak 1991). Mees (1995) illustrated the work of South Gaulish makers who are likely to have produced moulds.

An enormous amount of information, including whole and part designs and decorative details derived from vessels, found during excavations early this century at the manufacturing site of La Graufesenque is published by Hermet (1934). The illustrated designs and details are arranged by type or by period (based on judgement of an art historical nature), and are often difficult to relate to particular potters, whether bowl or mould makers. They do, however, provide a useful way of seeing the broad development of decorative schemes. The Oswald and Pryce discussion of form 29 (O&P, pp 66–77) also includes a general summary of decorative development.

The development of form 29 within the period c AD 43–85 can be seen by reference to a number of key deposits. Crucial here are two historically dated events: the burning of certain Romano-British towns by Boudicca in AD 61 and the eruption of Vesuvius which buried Pompeii and Herculaneum in AD 79. Material from pre-Boudiccan levels at Colchester, Verulamium and London will date c AD 43–60. That from Boudiccan fire deposits may be more precisely dated, particularly in the case of material from the Colchester 'pottery shops'. From Pompeii comes a 'hoard' of samian found in an unopened crate, and thus including decorative schemes current c AD 79 near the very end of form 29's currency.

For further discussion (and bibliography), particularly in connection with the Boudiccan Fires and the Pompeii Hoard, see below p 93ff.

The development of form 29 is shown in Fig 55. The upper vessel is a typical early form 29, with a rounded profile, rouletting on the central cordon and plant-derived decoration which tends to be formal and repetitive. If found in Britain, this vessel would probably date from the immediately post-conquest period.

The middle scheme retains the use of plant motifs, but the pattern is more elaborate, using more individual poinçons, and is less formal, if sometimes more crowded. The design would suit a date c AD 50–70.

The lower scheme still has some plant motifs, but small animal (and some human) figures have appeared. It is typical of the latest form 29s and would be early–mid Flavian in date (so c AD 70–85). The lower complete profile on p 39 shows a typical late shape with marked carination (change of direction part way up the body) and flaring rim. One would expect the lower design on Fig 55 to be on a bowl such as this.

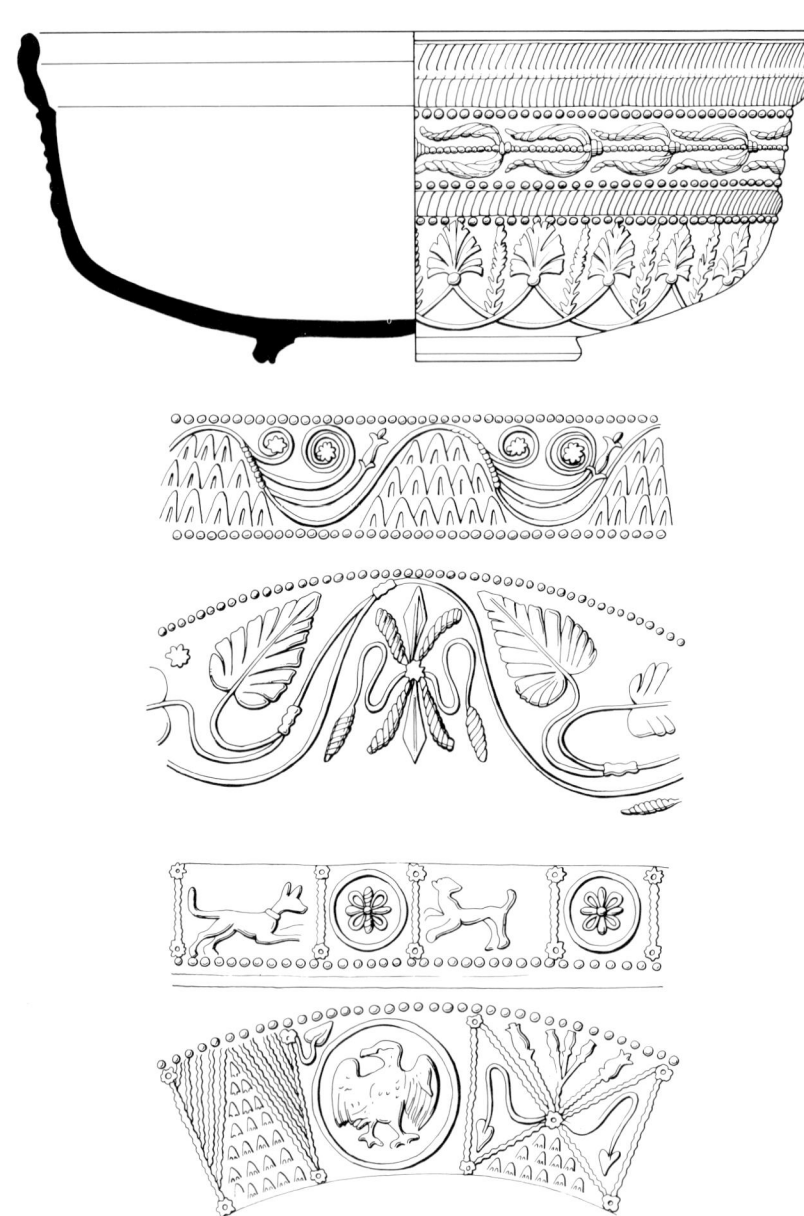

Fig 55 Form 29

76

FORM 30

The form is discussed above (p 42). The decoration is bounded at the top by an egg-and-tongue (ovolo) frieze. The decorative details are generally the same as those found on forms 29 and 37, but the schemes employed always tend to make full use of the deeper decorative zone.

The decoration of South Gaulish form 30s shows a similar progression, from solely plant-derived motifs, to those with animal and human content already noted in the case of form 29. However, they also tend to be more conservative in style than 29s, so that schemes of decoration which would be pre-Flavian on form 29 are often used on form 30 in the Flavian period. South Gaulish 30s also often show a higher degree of craftsmanship than contemporary 29s or 37s.

Later South Gaulish 30s and Central Gaulish examples of the form show decorative schemes comparable to those found on contemporary examples of form 37 (qv).

Hermet illustrates a wide range of South Gaulish 30s (1934, pls 69–77). Oswald and Pryce illustrate a range from all centres (O&P, pl VII–X & pp 86–93). Knorr, Mees, and Stanfield and Simpson do not illustrate form 30 separately, but examples are identifiable in their illustrations. See also comments on forms 29 and 37.

Two decorative schemes are illustrated in Fig 56 below, the left example, Flavian and South Gaulish, the right Antonine and Central Gaulish. Both show close similarities to schemes found on contemporary 37s.

 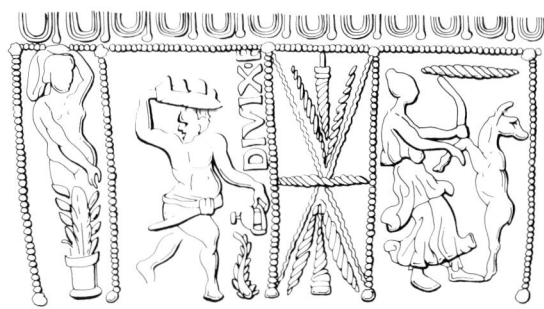

Fig 56 Form 30

FORM 37

The form is discussed above (p 47). The type emerged *c* AD 65–70. The Pompeii Hoard (Atkinson 1914) shows it to have been equal in popularity with form 29 by AD 79, but it must have eclipsed 29 shortly after this and was certainly the predominant decorated bowl form by *c* AD 85.

The decoration of the earliest 37s appears to be much influenced by that of contemporary 29s. It was divided into zones and used small *poinçons* designed for the narrow strips into which 29 was divided by its carination. Later 1st century vessels often continued to use zonal decoration but, as time went on, schemes (and poinçons) directly transposed from 29 give way to those which make more effective use of the uninterrupted surface of form 37. For example, on the earlier pieces, panel decoration will be arranged in zones bounded by continuous horizontal borders. Panel decoration remains popular to the end of South Gaulish export, but later examples are more likely to use panels of varying size and depth (cf Fig 57 middle). Use of the entire decorative area for a single scheme (free-style) is found among South Gaulish designs, but is comparatively rare.

The latest phase of South Gaulish production is notable for the comparatively slipshod nature of decoration and, particularly, of production. Perhaps as a result of pressure to increase production, moulds were often not cleaned properly, resulting in a loss of decorative detail on the pots. Vessels could also be removed from moulds before they were properly dried, giving blurred designs. This gives the impression of an industry in crisis or even in terminal decline.

When Central Gaul took over as the main exporting area, standards improved. Central Gaulish potters produced panel decoration, free-style (continuous scenes) and winding scroll designs largely unencumbered by styles and *poinçons* inherited from form 29. Les Martres potters tended to make finely detailed but crowded designs. Lezoux designs are generally more open. Divisions (eg panel borders) between design elements in the earlier part of the century (the Trajanic–Hadrianic period) are often, but by no means exclusively, wavy lines. Bead rows are much more frequent later (ie in the Antonine period) although this is only a very general 'rule of thumb'. Large 'advertisement' stamps were also a feature of Antonine production and the Antonine potters generally preferred large, bold designs, fairly well spaced, in comparison with the more crowded Trajanic and Hadrianic designs.

Form 37 ceased to be imported from Central Gaul at the close of the 2nd century. Antonine Central Gaulish samian production would appear to have been on a massive scale, and there is no sign of a decline in quality such as occurred with late South Gaulish production. It seems likely that importation ceased abruptly, for whatever reason, but large quantities of Central Gaulish samian will have remained in circulation in Britain, and will have survived either in use or residually well into the 3rd century.

East Gaulish 37s continued to be imported (from some factories) until the mid 3rd century. A very deep plain band below the bead of the rim is usually a late East Gaulish characteristic, as are heavy footrings. East Gaulish work is often characterized by the relatively small number of *poinçons* used but it is very difficult to generalize when one is dealing with a very large number of different centres of production, scattered over a wide area, not all of which were operating at the same time.

The vessels in Figs 57–66 are intended to provide pointers to work of the various centres but are no substitute for study of the more detailed literature listed below.

Hermet illustrates a range of South Gaulish form 37 designs (1934, pls 80–9). A range from all centres is shown by Oswald and Pryce (O&P, pls XI–XVIII & pp 95–105). Knorr illustrates some 37s (Knorr 1919 & 1952 *passim*) although, as late South Gaulish vessels are often unstamped by their makers, fewer are shown than one might expect. Mees (1995), however, includes many 37s produced by South Gaulish mouldmakers. Site reports can assist with Flavian examples, and useful material can be found in reports on early Caerleon, Brecon, and Newstead (see p 108ff for more bibliographical information) as well as Knorr's Rottweil report (1912) and that by Karnitsch for Ovilava (1959). Reports on the Bregenz Cellar find (Jacobs 1912) and on Holt (Grimes 1930) show a number of late South Gaulish 37s.

Stanfield and Simpson 1958 (S&S) and its revised French edition (S&S 1990) is the standard work for Central Gaulish vessels, illustrating collections of bowls (mostly form 37) bearing potters' stamps or other distinguishing features, and details of design for all the major Central Gaulish potters. For Les Martres-de-Veyre, additional information will be found in Terrisse 1968. Crucial for recent thinking on Central Gaulish dating is Hartley 1972 and S&S 1990.

When considering possible East Gaulish ware, it is worth bearing in mind that the most successful exporters to Britain were the potters of Rheinzabern, with those of La Madeleine, Lavoye, and Trier exporting smaller but still significant amounts. The literature for each production centre is listed on p 98 and, with identification of the specific source being the first priority, these must be the point of reference. Oswald's synthesis of figure types (1936–7), although not a substitute for the more detailed listings from certain specific centres, can be a useful starting point.

Fig 57 Form 37

FORM 37 a) South Gaulish (Fig 57)

The upper bowl shows the zoned decoration typical of South Gaulish bowls of the period *c* AD 70–90. The individual motifs (with the exception of the ovolo) could all appear on form 29, and the zonal arrangement gives the general appearance of a form 29 design transposed to the 'new' form with little alteration.

The middle bowl is a late South Gaulish design (*c* AD 90–110). It shows how the potters adapted to the hemispherical form. Some panels use most of the available decorative surface, thus breaking with the zoned effect of the upper example. Note also the use of large human figures.

The lower design is part of a 'free-style' scheme stamped in the mould by Germanus and probably later Flavian in date.

FORM 37 b) Les Martres-de-Veyre (Fig 58)

The mould makers of Les Martres were some of the most inventive of the Gaulish samian potters. They made use of numerous, often finely carved *poinçons*, both large and small. Their designs are generally tightly packed with detail. In the upper example (by the so-called 'Potter of the Rosette'), this can be seen from the large number of stamps used in each panel. In the lower 'free-style' design (by Drusus I), 'empty' space has been filled in with a few 'filler stamps'. Note the replacement of the ovolo with a substitute motif, a feature much more common among Les Martres designs than with those of later potters. Both vessels date *c* AD 100–120.

Fig 58 Form 37

FORM 37 c) Lezoux: Hadrianic to early Antonine (Fig 59)
The two schemes illustrated show both the debt of later makers to the
Trajanic potters of Les Martres and the way in which they moved away from
the Les Martres tradition. Fewer *poinçons* were used, for these schemes, than
in those of Les Martres and they are less crowded. They still, however, retain
something of the flavour of the earlier pieces through the use of small stamps
to infill otherwise empty spaces, and the overstamping of vertical borders. The
upper design is by Docilis (*c* AD 130–150), the lower by Ianuarius I (*c* AD
125–150).

Fig 59 Form 37

FORM 37 d) Lezoux: Cinnamus

Cinnamus was one of the most prolific of the Lezoux potters. He is illustrated here, both for this reason and as an example of early–mid Antonine style. The upper example shows a typical winding scroll design using large bold motifs with a few small infills. Notice the large 'advertisement' stamp. The lower design shows panel decoration. Notice how spaced out it appears when compared with the Les Martres examples in Fig 58 above. Cinnamus probably began work about AD 135 but these pieces belong to his main production period *c* AD 145–170.

Fig 60 Form 37

84

FORM 37 e) Lezoux: mid–late Antonine

The two decorative schemes illustrated are both by the potter Paternus (called Paternus II by Simpson in S&S 1990 to distinguish him from an earlier potter of the same name). The upper design shows a bold winding scroll popular in this period (but not restricted to it), while the lower is of the continuous 'free-style' type. Note the use of large 'advertisement' stamps.

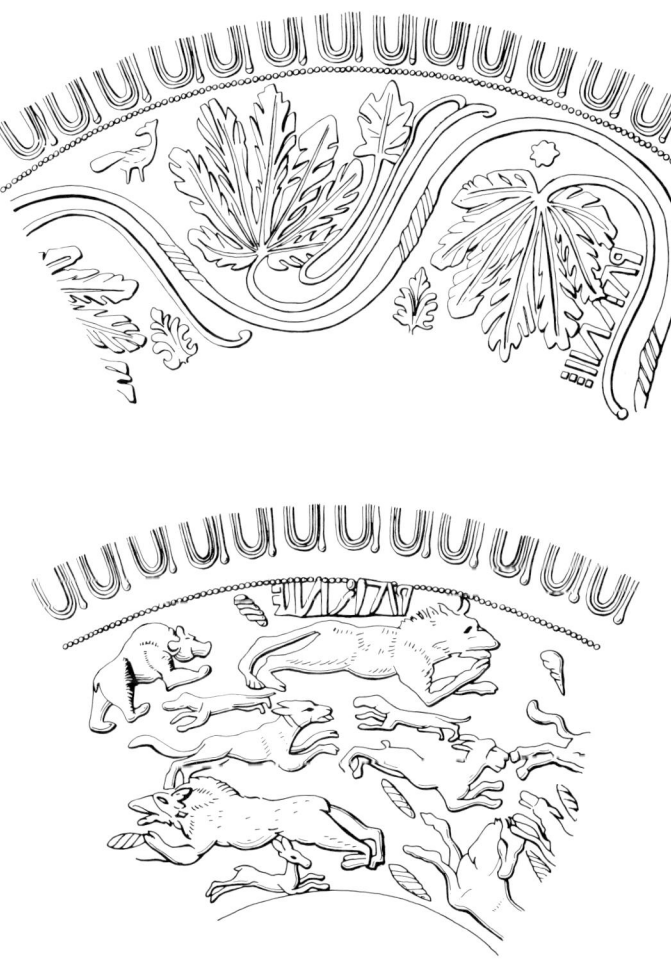

Fig 61 Form 37

f) Lezoux: forms 30 and 37

On this figure we have placed two panel designs by different potters and on different forms. The upper, on a form 37, is by Banvvs (*c* AD 160–195), a potter usually noted for his careless style. The lower is a form 30 by Doeccus (*c* AD 160–190) showing a rather neater version of the same type of design and, incidentally, illustrating how both 30 and 37 can carry similar designs.

Fig 62 Form 37

FORM 37 g) East Gaul: La Madeleine

La Madeleine is one of the earlier East Gaulish centres (exporting to Britain from about the mid-Hadrianic to mid-Antonine period), and its decoration shows similarities to that of contemporary Central Gaulish products. Note, however, the fondness for festoons and scrolls, and the general repetitiveness of designs using a limited range of *poinçons*.

Fig 63 Form 37

FORM 37 h) East Gaul: Rheinzabern

Rheinzabern was the most successful of the East Gaulish centres in terms of its exports to Britain. Figs 64–5 show a range of vessels produced during that exporting period (mid 2nd to mid 3rd century). The upper vessel on Fig 64 was produced by Cerialis V (late 2nd to early 3rd century) and the lower one by Janu[arius] II (late 2nd to mid 3rd century). Both schemes use fewer *poinçons* than one would expect in Central Gaulish designs of the same general type. A number of the elements are particular to Rheinzabern. The lack of border below the ovolo frieze is more common in East than in Central Gaul. Note also the lack of a tongue to the ovolo on the lower example.

Fig 64 Form 37

FORM 37 i) *East Gaul: Rheinzabern*

Three vessels are illustrated. The upper is in the style of Cerialis II (late 2nd to early 3rd century), the middle is by Comitialis VI (of similar date) and the lower is by Reginus I (Antonine). All show the rather spaced out character of many Rheinzabern designs and the limited range of *poinçons* employed. The lack of a border below the ovolo frieze is again noticeable.

Fig 65 Form 37

FORM 37 j) East Gaul: Trier

Trier was exporting to Britain from the Hadrianic period to the mid 3rd century. The two uppermost vessels illustrated here are from the so-called 'Werkstatt I', operating at the beginning of the exporting period. It is probably the idiosyncratic ovolos, the repetitive designs and the *poinçons* used for arcades and basal wreaths which would, in these cases indicate an East Gaulish (and Trier) origin. Later Trier pieces tend to use even fewer poinçons and to space the design elements further apart. The last design, which is by Paternianus (first half of the 3rd century) shows this tendency, although even more sparsely decorated Trier pots are possible.

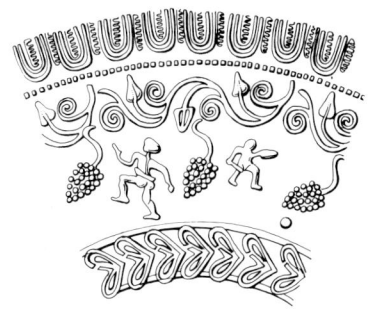

Fig 66 Form 37

Which potter? A guide to more detailed analysis

The occurrence in dated contexts of potters' stamps and, to a lesser extent, vessels with distinctive decoration, is the basis of samian chronology. Analysis is usually undertaken to try to identify the name of the bowl maker or mould maker (remembering that the two are not necessarily the same) and to use this to arrive at a date for the piece. Where vessels cannot be attributed to a potter, then the aim is to determine the date from the type of decorative scheme.

It is not easy to outline a procedure which will be valid in all cases, but a few basic questions can be suggested, together with more detailed procedures for the products of particular areas.

Preliminary questions

1 Is it stamped? Stamps usually occur in the basal interior, on the rim, in or under the decoration (see Fig 5). Signatures generally occur just below the decoration, but can occur within it; they can be very difficult to spot and a careful examination in oblique light of the zone between the decoration and the footring may be needed. Remember that not all stamps indicate the *mould* maker.

The standard work on stamps is still Oswald 1931. However, this work is soon to be superseded by the index currently being compiled at Leeds University by Brian Hartley and Brenda Dickinson, so that, at present, information on stamps should be sought from them. The Leeds index differs from Oswald 1931 in that it concentrates on individual stamps (ie the separate dies used), and is therefore able to distinguish between potters of the same name, as well as introducing considerably more precision into the dating process. Even so, Oswald can still be used with extreme caution, supplemented wherever possible by reference to some of the larger and more recent site reports, in which large numbers of stamps have been discussed. See also Hartley 1972, Knorr 1919 and 1952, S&S 1958 and 1990.

Signatures are also within the brief of the Leeds research. Some are discussed by Oswald (1927) South Gaulish signatures appear in Mees 1995, Central Gaulish signatures in S&S (cf particularly pl 169 in both editions).

2 What form is it? If it is form 29, it will almost certainly be South Gaulish and pre-AD 85. If it is form 37, it will probably be post AD 70. The sections dealing with form, above, give an indication of some other traits which may suggest a possible date range and/or source.

3 Is it South Gaulish, Central Gaulish or East Gaulish? See the section on fabric (p 13ff above). Sometimes a glance at the decoration will help. For example, if the vessel is a form 37, but the decoration looks like that often found on form 29, then it is probably a South Gaulish 37 of the Flavian period. Some decorative details or schemes are distinctive, for example the beaded cups and circles of dots used at Les Martres. The panels divided by bead rows, large medallions or large vine scrolls of Lezoux are easily spotted, as are the small circles used as 'fillers' in Lezoux decoration and some of the very open designs of East Gaul.

This will enable you to proceed to the 2nd stage of looking up the designs within the literature of the relevant area (see below) and will also give a very approximate date range. South Gaulish pieces will be pre *c* AD 110 (with form 29s pre *c* AD 85 and form 37s *c* AD 70–110), Central Gaulish pieces *c* AD 100–200 (with most Les Martres pieces *c* AD 100–120 and Lezoux post 120) and East Gaulish pieces will be *c* AD 125–250 (with further chronological division possible if the factory can be identified, see below). Remember that samian is as likely to be residual as any other artefact, and that pieces from the end of both Central Gaulish and East Gaulish production could have remained in use (sometimes repaired) well after the date of importation. Recent attempts to extend the date of the *importation* into Britain of Central Gaulish samian well into the 3rd century are not generally accepted by specialists.

Particular sources

SOUTH GAUL

Two parallel lines of enquiry are possible: the determination of individual potters and that of a general stylistic period.

The schemes of decoration associated with individual potters' stamps are gathered together in two works by R Knorr (*Knorr 1919* and *Knorr 1952*). These include both complete schemes of decoration and a breakdown of details (ie of the *poinçons* used). Particularly useful are the figures which gather together these details and list the potters using them (Knorr 1919, taf 5–13; Webster 1987, 45–62 for the details after Knorr but at full scale). For a compilation treating animal and 'human' figures only (from *all* centres of manufacture) see Oswald 1936–7. For decorative details, figure types and decorative schemes, see Hermet 1934, illustrating a vast range of material from La Graufesenque. The approach adopted by Hermet was, however, different from that of Knorr and Oswald. He divided the La Graufesenque material into phases of production, along lines which are essentially art historical and ascribed relatively little to individual potters.

With all South Gaulish work it is well to bear in mind that, where stamps occur, they are frequently from the bowls alone, ie they do not occur in the moulds but have been impressed after the bowls were made. *Stamps not certainly impressed into the moulds are, therefore, indicative only of bowl makers.* As has already been indicated, there is a strong possibility of a 'trade' both in poinçons and moulds. Specific details often occur in the work marketed by several bowl makers, indicating a common source of *poinçons* for their moulds. Likewise, closely similar schemes appear in the work of different bowl makers, indicating a common source of moulds. As a result it is rarely possible to identify the actual potter producing a bowl, but only what are, in effect, the trading connections of those supplying the poinçons and/or moulds reaching his (and other) workshops. Current work is directed towards identifying mould makers and their trading connections and an important new compendium of mould makers' work is to be found in Mees 1995. However, some attention to dating by decorative style is also advised.

Fortunately, there are some fairly well dated contexts (and a very few extremely well dated ones) which allow us to date the general development of South Gaulish decorative schemes. Of course, almost everything from a securely British context will be post AD 43 and this is worth bearing in mind. For the succeeding decades the following groups are crucial:

1 Material from the Boudiccan burning of Romano-British towns in AD 61. Of especial use is the material from the Colchester 'pottery shops' destroyed in the Boudiccan sack of Colchester (Hull 1958, 152–6, 198–202). The vessels from the shops will have been on sale at the time of the burning, so it is fairly certain that they were made and imported only a short time before. There is not the same certainty about other Boudiccan fire deposits (eg Verulamium, Frere 1972, 218–23, Frere 1984, 181–97 *passim*, or the less well documented London collection), but they still have an upper date of AD 61 which is of considerable use.

2 Pompeii. The town was buried in the eruption of Vesuvius in AD 79. All samian from the town will, therefore, predate this. Of particular interest is the so-called Pompeii Hoard, a group of samian apparently assembled in North Italy (as it was accompanied by a number of north Italian lamps), and still in its original crate awaiting unpacking when buried in AD 79 (cf Atkinson 1914). This collection falls within the same category as the Colchester 'pottery shop' material, in that it must have been made only a short time before the catastrophic (and well documented) event which led to its burial.

We lack such reliable groups after AD 79 and, indeed, the pottery of *c* AD 80–110 is not well represented in Knorr's work cited above. However, there is sufficient material from Flavian sites, particularly in Wales and north Britain, to go part way towards making up for this. Newstead (with a terminal date c AD 105) is most useful. Dickinson and Hartley (in Monaghan 1993) illustrate vessels from the early years of the York Fortress (c AD 71–100, but many are from the first half of this range) while Zienkiewicz 1992 illustrates a collection from the very beginning of the Caerleon Fortress (so presumably c AD 75–80). Northwich (Wild 1971) and Holt (Grimes 1930) contain useful late South Gaulish collections.

Many of the larger site reports and catalogues include a good range of South Gaulish material. These will be found listed together below (p 109). Good places to start looking are the reports on Fishbourne, Verulamium, Usk, Carlisle, York, Richborough, and Caerleon, and the large early catalogues from Colchester (May 1930) and Silchester (May 1916). Walters 1908 includes many London pieces, and a small amount appears in Pryce and Oswald 1928 and RCHM 1928 (but see also Marsh 1979a). Among foreign reports that on Ovilava (Karnitsch 1959) is particularly useful for Flavian material, while the groups from Neronian Narbonne (Fiches *et al* 1978), and the Bregenz cellar (Jacobs 1912) contain useful small collections. The Knorr reports on material from Cannstatt and Rottweil (1905, 1912) should also be noted.

Although La Graufesenque was the largest exporter of South Gaulish samian, there were some other exporting centres, of which Banassac and Montans were the most important, although their work, apart from some late Montans ware of the Hadrianic–Antonine period, rarely reached Britain. For the work of the Montans potters see Martin 1974, Labrousse 1975 and Simpson 1976. For Banassac see Hoffmann 1988 and Mees 1995, 101–12, Taf 226–45.

For a review of all South Gaulish centres with extensive bibliographies see Bémont & Jacob 1986. This work shows many of the plain forms produced at the various centres. Its treatment of decorated ware is largely restricted to a few selective illustrations.

CENTRAL GAUL (Les Martres-de-Veyres and Lezoux)
With Central Gaulish work it is rather easier to determine the names of individual potters or (as is the case with many Les Martres pieces), to identify the style of particular mould makers. This is probably because the industry was less fragmented and the making of *poinçons*, moulds and bowls appears often to have taken place within the same firm, although the selling of moulds between workers and even to other factories (as evidenced by the presence of Lezoux moulds at Vichy and Lubie) certainly did take place. For Central Gaulish work, the suggested procedure is as follows:

1 The ovolo. The egg-and-tongue frieze at the top of the decoration tended to be particular to one potter or to a related group of potters. As such it deserves to be looked at first of all, although it has to be said that worn, smudged or indistinct ovolos abound and study of the ovolo has, on occasion, to be set aside in favour of clearer details. However, assuming a clearly impressed ovolo, the first reference should be to Rogers 1974 (section B), although this can often be supplemented by the text-figures in S&S. The 1990 edition of S&S includes cross-references to Rogers. It should be noted that Rogers includes many drawings made from moulds, marked 'M' in the text (as opposed to drawings from bowls, marked 'B'). Mould details are not only often more detailed than they appear on the bowls but will also be larger due to the shrinkage of bowls before and during firing. It is normally reckoned that a detail could lose up to one tenth of its size in this way.

2 Figure types and decorative details. These are the result of the application of individual *poinçons* to the moulds. So types and details are the *poinçons* as revealed by the finished bowls (or sometimes the moulds). For *animate* types Déchelette 1904 and Oswald 1936–7 should be used (Oswald's collection is more extensive; Déchelette sometimes has more detail, is artistically more accomplished and sometimes varies slightly from Oswald). It is important to remember that the texts of Déchelette and Oswald were written long before the publication of the work of Stanfield and Simpson. Therefore, for more information on those types appearing on stamped vessels, it is necessary to refer to Stanfield & Simpson (S&S) p 285ff (the chart is *not* repeated in S&S 1990). For the Trajanic potters, many of whom did not stamp their names in their pots, S&S p 58ff is essential (again not repeated in S&S 1990). Inanimate elements will be found in Rogers 1974, although, again, care must be taken to distinguish drawings taken from moulds and those from bowls (see ovolos above).

Ideally, having considered ovolo and decorative elements, you should have a series of lists showing potters known to have used the individual elements of the design. There should also be some names recurring in most or all of the lists and it is at this stage that it is useful to consider the style of the bowl in question and, in particular, to find out if the style matches that of a potter known to use the elements present. It is also worth remembering that some (usually small) decorative details are particular to specific potters or to a small group of potters. The texts in Rogers 1974 and S&S should identify these elements.

3 Decorative schemes associated with the stamps of particular potters or in particularly distinctive styles are gathered together in Stanfield and Simpson 1958 (S&S) and its revised edition, S&S 1990 (which has some additional plates of schemes). This work is divided between the Trajanic potters (pls 1–61) who were mainly those working at Les Martres-de-Veyre, and later potters (S&S, pls 62–166; S&S 1990, pls 62–166, 170–5) who were mainly those working at Lezoux. For each potter there is a collection of illustrated designs and accompanying text with, in many cases, text-figures of decorative details. For the Les Martres potters, S&S can be supplemented by Terrisse 1968.

In all cases, it is necessary to remember that only the occurrence of stamps or signatures certainly impressed into the mould will indicate the mould maker, and there are certainly a number of potters illustrated who acquired their moulds from other workshops. The Les Martres potters, in particular, rarely stamped their work, but when they did, it was after moulding, so that there is not necessarily any correlation between identifiable styles and named potters. The realisation of this led Rogers to divide the Trajanic potters by mould style (cf Rogers 1974, 22, and the note on names below). S&S 1990 uses the Rogers nomenclature.

4 Dating. The historical phases of the northern frontier in Britain provide a basis for the division of the 2nd century and thus an opportunity to assess the working periods of individual samian potters. However, the problems of relating historical events and their archaeological contexts, particularly in the later Antonine period, must be borne in mind. It is the northern evidence, as seen in 1958 (ie with an AD 197 destruction of Hadrian's Wall), which lay behind the dating originally proposed by Stanfield and Simpson. This should be supplemented by the revised edition (S&S 1990) and its bibliography, where necessary. Also extremely useful is Hartley 1972 for seeing potters in relation to the datable Wall markets and for its insights into recent thinking. Recent attempts to lengthen the exporting period of Lezoux samian beyond the late 2nd century have not found favour with most specialists.

As well as the northern evidence, there are a number of useful collections resulting from fires within Romano-British towns, where the components can be shown to have been on sale or to have been bought at or near the date of the fire. Thus the Wroxeter Gutter Find (Atkinson 1942, 127–46 & pls 32–37 *passim*) consists of vessels on sale from stalls in the Forum portico at the time of a mid-Antonine fire. A comparable early Antonine group comes from the

Castleford 'pottery shop' similarly destroyed in a fire (Hartley & Dickinson in press). Other material from the Wroxeter Fire (Atkinson 1942, 147–73, pls 32–7 *passim* & pls 38–43), like that from the Antonine fire at Verulamium (Frere 1972, 254–62) will include much material actually in use at the time of the fires.

Note: the names of Central Gaulish potters.
The names of potters used in S&S, Terrisse 1968, Rogers 1974 and S&S 1990 vary slightly. Some un-named potters were given X-numbers by Stanfield. The names of some of these have now been identified (eg Stanfield's X-3 is now called Drusus I). Other potters, known from imperfectly read stamps or named after elements of their decoration in S&S have now been re-named as a result of new information. Thus potter X-4 or Cocatus of S&S is now identified as Igocatus, and the 'small-S potter' of S&S is now known to have been called Cettus. The GI Vibius of S&S is now thought to have been called Geminus. As already stated, Rogers (1974) reconsidered the Trajanic potters catalogued by Stanfield and Simpson. As a result of considering the likely authorship of moulds, he extended the X-potter names, dividing some of the S&S units in the process. His re-ascriptions are to be found in Rogers 1974, 22. On the same principle, Rogers lists other mould makers by X-numbers and P-numbers, but full details of these potters awaits a future volume of his catalogue. For the latest nomenclature see S&S 1990.

EAST GAUL
There are many East Gaulish factories and the first problem is to find the source of any individual piece. It is, however, worth bearing in mind that East Gaulish wares as a whole form only a small percentage of site finds in Britain and that distribution is biased towards the south, the south-east and the northern military zone. Furthermore, most of the East Gaulish ware that reached Britain from the later 2nd century onwards came from Rheinzabern, although there was a significant importation from Trier and, at an earlier (Hadrianic–Antonine) date, from La Madeleine.

Publications which include figure types, decorative details and decorative schemes exist for many of the East Gaulish factories. Initial identification is, however, made easier by the inclusion of many East Gaulish figure types in Oswald 1936–7.

After the factory has been identified, analysis is much the same as for Central Gaulish ware, but with the appropriate books as follows:

Rheinzabern	Ricken & Fischer 1963 (ovolos & figure types)
	Ludowici & Ricken 1948 (schemes)
	Bittner 1986 (dating)
La Madeleine	Ricken 1934; Folzer 1913
Trier	Huld-Zetsche 1972 & 1993; Folzer 1913; Huld-Zetsche 1971 (3rd century plain ware)
The Argonne	Chenet & Gaudron 1955; Oswald 1945
Blickweiler	Knorr & Sprater 1927
Chemery, Bouchporn &	
the Satto-Saturninus factory	Delort 1953; Lutz 1970 & 1977
Heiligenberg	Forrer 1911
Sinzig	Fischer 1969

There are a number of useful site collections which include East Gaulish ware. These include Butzbach (Muller 1968), Cannstatt (Knorr 1905), Lauriacum and Ovilava (Karnitsch 1955 and 1959 although the dating given in these needs to be treated with caution as far as the later Rheinzabern potters is concerned), Saalburg and Zugmantel (Ricken 1934), Zwammerdam (Haalebos 1977) and St Magnus House, London (Bird 1986).

It should be noted that the available evidence and chronology of the Rheinzabern potters has been much discussed (cf Simon 1968, Bernhard 1981, and Bittner 1986). The best summary of this in English is in Bird 1986, but much concerning close dating of these potters remains in doubt (cf Mees 1993).

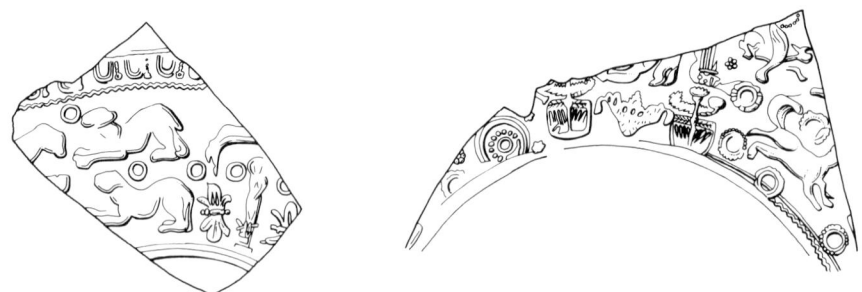

Figure 67 Samian by the Aldgate-Pulborough Potter. Note the crowded designs and the unusually small figures (the result of copying details from already fired bowls).

There were clearly some attempts during the 2nd century to produce samian in Britain, but the distribution of such wares is very limited and really only of localised interest. It is generally sufficient to be aware of the existence of such work, rather than to be familiar with its characteristics.

A number of potters producing samian are known from Colchester (see Hull 1963, 21–34 & 43–74, but also Storey *et al* 1989 for evidence that Hull's Potter C is, in fact, imported samian from Sinzig). There was also one operating in south east England within an area bounded by Silchester, London, and the Sussex coast. The latter is the so-called 'Aldgate-Pulborough potter' (see Simpson 1952; Webster 1975; Bennett 1978; Marsh 1979b). The work of all these British potters, although derived from continental work, is highly distinctive and their fabrics unlike those of continental producers.

6   Dealing with a site collection

So far we have concentrated on the identification of individual sherds. However, the writing of a samian report will probably involve consideration of a large number of sherds within a site assemblage which includes many classes of artefact. It is necessary, therefore, to think about the best way to deal with large quantities of samian as a site collection.

Obviously, there may be considerable variations between assemblages from different sites, and the procedures to be adopted will have to be altered accordingly. A number of general suggestions can, however, be made:

1   In preparing any samian report, the first question should always be 'What aspects of the history of the site do I expect the samian to help elucidate?' It is likely that the answers will fall into two categories, the chronological and the socio-economic. The samian will form an important element in establishing site chronology, because it is often fairly closely datable. However, it will also play a part in establishing the trading connections of the site, and the social status of its Roman owner.

2   For any report, it is always a good idea to begin with a brief look at the entire assemblage. This will probably provide a rough idea of the date-range. It will also indicate whether you are dealing with large pieces or small abraded ones, and probably show if joins between sherds in different contexts can be expected. It will also give an overall impression of the amount of decorated ware to be expected and its state of preservation. The strategy to be adopted will depend on such first impressions. Small abraded fragments will yield less information than large well-preserved pieces. Pursuit of joins is time-consuming but necessary if likely to prove productive. Decorated ware takes a good deal longer to report upon than plain ware, but often lends itself to greater chronological precision.

3   The next move should probably be to arrange the collection in an order helpful to both 'reporter' and excavator (usually context or perhaps phase order), and then go through the entire collection making notes. It is probably best at this stage to record all the vessels in each context by form number and source (ie South Gaulish, Central Gaulish etc), to note any obvious joins between contexts and to give an approximate date to all decorated pieces. This will provide an outline archive report, and will also

indicate residual vessels (eg those from earlier periods dredged from their original contexts by building operations or similar disruptive activities and now occurring with later pieces). It may well be that such residual pieces will not need much further work on them as they will add little to the chronological picture. This is also the stage to make some preliminary general observations (eg 'decorated ware seems unduly scarce'; 'cups seem more plentiful than usual') such as can be substantiated (or otherwise) through further work. If the archive is to form part of the site records (as it should), it will probably be helpful to record all decorated ware with mounted rubbings (the process of rubbing is described at the end of this chapter).

4   Once a fairly detailed picture of the collection has been gained, it is time to consider the samian within the general context of the site as a whole. Here, communication with the excavator is important, as what can be done will depend very much on the amount of site information available and the current state of other post-excavation work. Unnecessary work can be saved if two types of information are available: a) a firm stratigraphic order; b) preliminary (or final) reports on other classes of artefact (eg coins or coarse pottery). Discussion with the excavator should reveal just what he expects the samian report to tell him. It may be that he is relying upon the samian to allow him to place certain contexts into their appropriate phases. It is always useful to know how much weight the excavator wishes to place on your dating of specific contexts. Certainly, the more general discussion there is between the excavator and all specialists, the better will be the final report. From the point of view of the samian 'reporter', the discussion should enable him or her to do three things:

i)   Put the samian in a stratigraphic sequence which agrees with that used by the excavator in his 'structural' report, making cross-reference easier.

ii) Identify further residual elements. Once other dating evidence is available some contexts will be seen to contain samian which is entirely residual. It is, for instance, quite common for late Antonine samian to appear scattered through 3rd and even 4th century contexts.

iii) Identify those sherds (usually decorated pieces) requiring detailed analysis and close dating in a published catalogue which provides the essential dating evidence for the site. It is worth bearing in mind that precise dating is not necessarily given solely by the latest piece. To give an example: a level which contains ten sherds of Les Martres samian of *c* AD 100–120 and one piece of Lezoux of *c* AD 120–145 must surely date from soon after 120; however that date is not given solely by the one

Hadrianic piece, but by consideration of all eleven pieces. As a result the catalogue would need to include at least some of the Les Martres pieces to establish the point. Although you will generally be dating the end of periods of occupation, in the case of the first period, at least, it will be necessary to establish the beginning of all occupation and this may require a fuller publication of first period sherds.

5   There may be a few pieces which have an interest beyond that of site chronology. Some sherds may, for instance, extend the range of decorative schemes or details known to have been used by individual potters. Such items of intrinsic interest will be few, but need to be set aside for inclusion in the published catalogue. Samian stamps are also usually treated in this way, even if they are not chronologically significant, as they extend the information known about individual potters, if only in terms of the distribution of their wares.

We have so far concentrated on work which provides the basis for a pottery archive and a published catalogue. With a small collection, it may be that little more can be done. However, the larger the collection and the better the stratigraphic differentiation, the more likely it is that other questions can be answered. Many of these questions will involve quantitative analysis of the collection.

6   By this stage, the 'reporter' will have the basis of a publishable catalogue. In terms of chronology, he or she should already have most of the information, however it is worth bearing in mind that the approach suggested has emphasised the date, but not the intensity of occupation. Intensity of activity is more likely to be gauged by counting the material in some way. Similarly, socio-economic questions may well have a quantitative element. To use an example already given: it may be that there appears to be less decorated ware or more cups than usual. Before suggesting a lower status abode (for the site with less decorated ware), or an inn (for the cups), it would be as well to quantify the elements involved (and, of course, to consult the excavator for corroboration from other evidence).

The basic archive of all vessels already made (stage 3 above) should be sufficient to enable a simple 'minimum vessel count' to be made, ie to determine the minimum number of vessels of any given category likely to have been present in a phase or on the site as a whole. This may be all that is required and, before doing anything further, it is probably worth asking the excavator whether other methods of quantification are in use for other classes of artefact. On a large site, or a site within a larger unit (eg one on a much excavated town) it may be that more sophisticated statistical methods are in use, and it would be desirable to integrate the samian quantification with these.

It is not the purpose here to expound on statistical methods of quantification. Readers should, however, be aware of the work of Orton and Tyers (1990) whose 'pie-slice' quantification looks, at the time of writing, as if it will replace other methods on large sites. Like most other methods it depends on calculating so-called estimated vessel equivalents (EVES). This is usually done from rims only and consists of placing the sherd on a rim-scale and noting the percentage of rim present. This percentage is recorded along with other details of the vessel. At the end of the exercise the percentages in any given category can be added up and expressed on the assumption that one EVE is 100%. The statisticians are confident that this forms a better basis for comparing site with site than a simple minimum vessel count. Even so, common sense indicates that to produce the reasonably large number of EVES necessary to have quantities capable of meaningful comparison will involve analysis of very large assemblages indeed and that unless there are such numbers (and on most sites there are not), then less sophisticated methods may be more applicable.

7 General comments, if possible backed up by quantification, perhaps in a chart or histogram, can then form an introduction to the catalogue to be published. This is the place for outline statements of chronology and for socio-economic deductions. The catalogue should then detail and illustrate the pieces selected. The original archive lists (and perhaps some of the detail of quantification) form part of the site archive.

The emphasis is thus on producing a report which is as concise as possible. The method must be efficient in terms of time. It is suggested that this will be achieved most easily by integrating the writing of the report as closely as possible with the analysis of the site as a whole and of its entire artefact assemblage. The more isolated the samian reporter, the more unnecessary (and therefore time-consuming) work will be done and the greater the danger of a final report which is less relevant than it might have been.

Recording decorated samian by rubbing

In final published reports decorated samian is generally recorded by drawings, although in some, usually German or Dutch works, casts from latex moulds are photographed. Such methods are very time-consuming and expensive, and often it is not practical to use them for recording all the samian within a collection. There is, however, a method of rapid recording used in Britain for archive and research purposes which is ideal for use with large collections either for a basic catalogue or for other record purposes. This is rubbing using graphite.

The method is very similar to that commonly used for recording church brasses, although the materials used are different. The paper has to be thin, capable of taking up the irregularities of relief decoration and with a matt finish that will not slip too easily on a glossy surface. Tissue paper meets these requirements and it has been found that the tissue used for cigarettes is particularly good. In small pieces, such paper is, of course, available from most tobacconists. Such 'cigarette papers' with gummed strips, are particularly useful for small details or stamps. Decorated sherds, however, require larger areas of paper and this has to be obtained from a commercial supplier. Rizla of Severn Road, Treforest Industrial Estate, Pontypridd, Mid Glamorgan, CF37 5SP will supply 17g paper (their 'Mascotte' tissue paper) in quantities of 300 sheets (520mm × 735mm).

The best medium for producing the image on the paper seems to be graphite, and this is available at varying grades from engineering suppliers (it is a commercial lubricant). Powdered graphite is best avoided as it does not produce as good an image and tends to blow about which could be a health hazard. Flake graphite is to be preferred. Small/medium flakes (Foliac grade 2a) are the easiest to use but the larger flakes (Foliac grade 2b) are preferred by some. Flake graphite can be bought in half or one kilogram tins. One tin will last a lifetime.

When rubbing, it is important to keep the paper from slipping on the sherd and it helps to have enough paper to wrap around it. In very hot conditions, it may be necessary to keep both pot and paper away from the sun as very hot pots and over-dry paper do not give good rubbings. However, this is rarely a problem in British conditions! Rubbing is usually done by dipping a finger or thumb in a small pile of graphite and rubbing it on the surface of the paper. The decoration in relief will soon appear. Faint elements of the decoration can be 'heightened' by careful rubbing.

Once rubbings have been made they should be trimmed, mounted on paper or card and 'fixed' with a spray in the same way as soft pencil drawings. Once mounted (and labelled) they can be reproduced using a photocopier and thus form a handy record for use in archive reports or for individual research purposes. Good rubbings are also capable of being 'scanned' into computer records.

7 Books

In any pottery study, it is at least as important to have a knowledge of where to find information (ie a command of the literature) as it is to have a knowledge of the actual pottery and its forms.

The literature of samian is vast and multilingual. As a result, even a modest bibliography, such as that given at the end of this work can be very offputting. In an effort to make it easier to use, some of the more important books have been selected and divided below by subject. Some personal judgement as to the degree of importance of books within certain categories will also be apparent.

Introductions

The best introductions are **Hartley 1969** and **Johns 1977**. Some aspects treated in these two works are amplified in **Bulmer 1980**. A convenient introduction, albeit aimed at a more general audience is **Bédoyère 1988** which concentrates mainly on decorated ware. **Webster 1987** is a forerunner of the present work.

Plain ware

The basic work is **Oswald & Pryce 1920 (O&P)**. Regrettably, since the publication of **O&P**, far less plain samian has appeared in published reports. **Hartley 1969** and **Hartley 1972** are important for comments on specific types. **Ettlinger *et al* 1990** brings together information on Arretine forms so is useful for seeing the origin of many Gallic samian forms. **Hawkes & Hull 1947** contains some early material from Camulodunum. **Manning 1993** contains a range of plain ware from the Neronian Fortress at Usk. **Bird 1986** includes a range of later types. Works on individual manufacturing centres often contain some plain ware and are particularly useful for types which are unusual away from their place of origin; **Bémont & Jacob 1986** gathers together information from most of the Gaulish centres and **Bird 1993** for 3rd century East Gaulish forms.

Decorated ware
General

With decorated ware, in particular, it is important to look at the date of publication of the various works. More recent publications will, to a certain extent, modify statements made in the earlier works.

O&P (1920) contains a general summary of decorative development. Figure types are to be found in **Oswald 1936–7** which amplifies but does not altogether replace **Déchelette 1904**. **Oswald 1931** is still the only general compendium of potters' stamps, but is superseded by the Leeds Index (see p 92).

South Gaul

Knorr 1919 and **Knorr 1952** are essential. **Hermet 1934** has many designs and a useful set of decorative details but, in general, divides decorative schemes by broad chronological period, rather than by potter. The decorative details collected together by Knorr (1919, Textbild 6–13) are redrawn at full scale and numbered in **Webster 1987**, but remember that Knorr concentrated on stamped *bowls* and that the bowl maker was not necessarily the mould maker. For the identification of potters likely to have been making moulds and a compendium of their work **Mees 1995** is essential.

Important for dating are:
1 The Boudiccan Fire deposits, particularly the Colchester 'pottery shops', (**Hull 1958**, 152–5, 198–202, and Verulamium, (**Frere 1972**, 218–23). **Frere 1984** also contains some early material although the fire deposit is not as clearly divided as in the 1972 volume. **Niblett 1985** also includes some important early material, but requires a print-out of the microfiche to be used effectively.
2 The Pompeii Hoard (**Atkinson 1914**).

Also useful is **Knorr 1912** and, for Neronian decorated ware, **Manning 1993** and **Fiches** *et al* **1978**. The latest South Gaulish work is not well represented in **Knorr 1919** and **1952** and, for this, the following sites may be useful: Ovilava (**Karnitsch 1959**), the Bregenz cellar (**Jacobs 1912**), large collections from British sites of Flavian foundation such as Caerleon (**Nash-Williams 1929** and **1932**), Brecon (**Wheeler 1926**) and Newstead (**Curle 1911**). Holt (**Grimes 1930**) contains some of the later South Gaulish pieces.

For Montans ware see **Labrousse 1975** and **Simpson 1976**.
For Banassac see **Hoffmann 1988**.

Central Gaul

Essential is **Stanfield & Simpson 1958** (**S&S**) and its revised French version, **S&S 1990**; also **Terrisse 1968** (for Les Martres-de-Veyre) and **Rogers 1974** (for inanimate decorative details, complementing Oswald who dealt with the animate details). **Hartley 1972** is important for dating and for the comments, particularly on Cinnamus. **Déchelette 1904** is a useful supplement to **Oswald 1936–7** for figure types. For the work of Cinnamus see also **Simpson & Rogers 1969**.

East Gaulish

As Rheinzabern is the most important source of East Gaulish samian found in Britain, the important works are **Ludowici & Ricken 1948** for decorative schemes and **Ricken & Fischer 1963** for both animate and inanimate types (supplementing Oswald 1936–7). An English summary of Rheinzabern dating is given in **Bird 1986** which also includes one of the largest number of East Gaulish decorated samian published from a British site. The bibliography of the other factories is given on p 99. Site reports with large amounts of East Gaulish samian include Ovilava (**Karnitsch 1959**), Lauriacum (**Karnitsch 1955**), Saalburg (**Ricken 1934**), Neuss (**Schonberger & Simon 1966**), Langenhain (**Simon & Kohler 1992**) and Asciburgium (**Vanderhoeven 1974**).

The wider application of samian studies

Here, we have concerned ourselves with basic identification and dating, but those who would like to see how samian can be used for a more general study are recommended to two works: **Hartley 1972**, which uses samian as an historical tool to help disentangle the chronology of Roman Scotland; and **Marsh 1981** which looks at the samian industry in relation to a major consumer, the city of London. For the application of statistical studies to a body of samian information see Paul Tyers in **Manning 1993**. For samian as an element in Roman pottery studies as a whole see **Greene 1992**.

Site reports and collections

The following reports on site assemblages or collections are some which contain reasonably large amounts of samian often combined with chronological divisions within the site. They are suggested as the starting point for any site-based search for specific parallels. They are listed in the order in which they appear in the Bibliography at the back of this book. As a general rule works have been cited according to the author of the entire book or article rather than according to the author of the samian report. Where the author of the samian report is not apparent this has been added in square brackets after the site name. Some comments on the strengths of each report have been added.

Atkinson, 1942	Wroxeter. Particularly useful for the material associated with the mid-Antonine Fire.
Bird, 1986	London (St Magnus House). An important waterfront group including 3rd century East Gaulish wares.
Bushe-Fox, 1926; 1928	Richborough (I–II). The site was occupied throughout the Roman period and has a wide range of samian.
Bushe-Fox, 1932	Richborough (III) [Davies Pryce]. See Bushe-Fox 1926.
Bushe-Fox, 1949	Richborough (IV) [Davies Pryce, Hayter]. See Bushe-Fox 1926.
Curle, 1911	Newstead. Flavian and Antonine occupation.
Cunliffe, 1968	Richborough (V) [Dickinson, Hartley, Pierce, Simpson]. See Bushe-Fox 1926.
Cunliffe, 1971	Fishbourne [Dannell]. Useful 1st century material.
Edwards & Webster, 1985; 1988	Ribchester [Wild]. Flavian to Antonine.

Frere, 1972; 1984	Verulamium [Hartley & Dickinson]. Particularly important for the Boudiccan and mid-Antonine Fire groups.
Grimes, 1930	Holt [Pryce & Oswald]. Useful for late Flavian material.
Haalebos, 1977	Zwammerdam. A large site collection.
Hartley, 1985	Inchtuthil. The site was occupied only from the early to mid 80s so that this small collection is closely dated.
Hawkes & Hull, 1947	Camulodunum [with Davies Pryce]. A mid-1st century collection.
Holbrook & Bidwell, 1991	Exeter [Dickinson & Dannell]. Useful 1st century material.
Hulde-Zetsche, 1971	Trier. A useful group of 3rd century plain ware.
Hull, 1958	Colchester. Mainly important for the 'pottery shop' groups dating from the Boudiccan Fire.
Karnitsch, 1955	Lauriacum. A site collection with useful East Gaulish material.
Karnitsch, 1959	Ovilava. A site collection, mainly useful for the later Flavian South Gaulish and the East Gaulish elements.
Knorr, 1905	Cannstatt. Plentiful East Gaulish ware.
Knorr, 1907; 1912	Rottweil. The 1907 work has mainly South and East Gaulish ware; the 1912 work has mid to late 1st century South Gaulish ware.
Manning, 1993	Usk [Johns]. Important for the material from the Neronian to early Flavian fortress.

Mary, 1967	Neuss. A large South Gaulish collection.
May, 1916	Silchester. A large town collection of all periods but the photographed reproduction is of variable quality.
May & Hope, 1917	Carlisle. A useful addition to the more recent publications (McCarthy 1990, Taylor 1991)
May, 1930	Colchester. A large town collection.
McCarthy, 1990	Carlisle [Dickinson]. A Flavian and 2nd century assemblage.
Mees, 1990	Vechten. Mid and late 1st century wares are particularly well represented.
Monaghan, 1993	York [Dickinson & Hartley]. Important for the material from the early fortress (founded AD 71+).
Muller, 1968	Butzbach. Some South and Central Gaulish material but important for the range of East Gaulish wares from various centres.
Niblett, 1985	Colchester [Dannell]. Important Boudiccan fire material.
Oelmann, 1914	Niederbieber. Useful East Gaulish material, including plain ware.
Perrin, 1990	York [Hartley & Dickinson]. Second and 3rd century decorated ware.
Ricken, 1934	Saalburg & Zugmantel. Important for its analysis of East Gaulish ware.
Robertson, 1975	Birrens [Wild]. Useful for its 2nd century East Gaulish ware.

Simon & Kohler, 1992

Langenhain. A cellar deposit from outside the fort which includes Rheinzabern and Trier ware of the 3rd century.

Smith, 1907; 1909

Pudding Pan Rock. A later 2nd century wreck notable for its plain ware.

Taylor, 1991

Carlisle [Dickinson]. Flavian and later decorated ware.

Vanderhoeven, 1974–8

Asciburgium. The fascicules are divided by source as follows: 1974, Central and East Gaulish (Heft 2, Decorated; Heft 3, Stamps); 1976 & 1978, South Gaulish.

Wacher & McWhirr, 1982

Cirencester [Hartley & Dickinson]. First century ware including the important fort ditch deposit of *c* AD 55–65.

Walke, 1965

Straubing. Later South Gaulish ware with Central and East Gaulish ware (including plain ware).

Walters, 1908

British Museum. A large and important collection but reported upon too early to contain useful analysis. However, for a division of Walter's Central Gaulish material by potter, see Simpson nd.

Wheeler, 1930

London [Davies Pryce, Birley]. Reference to the earliest material should only be made in conjunction with Marsh 1979a.

Summary charts

The period figures below show a selection of forms which would be regarded as *typical* of each period. The figures are not intended to show *all* forms current in any one period, nor are they intended to indicate that any particular form is restricted *only* to the period in which it appears below. Rather the groupings are intended to show forms which, if found together, would suggest the dating given.

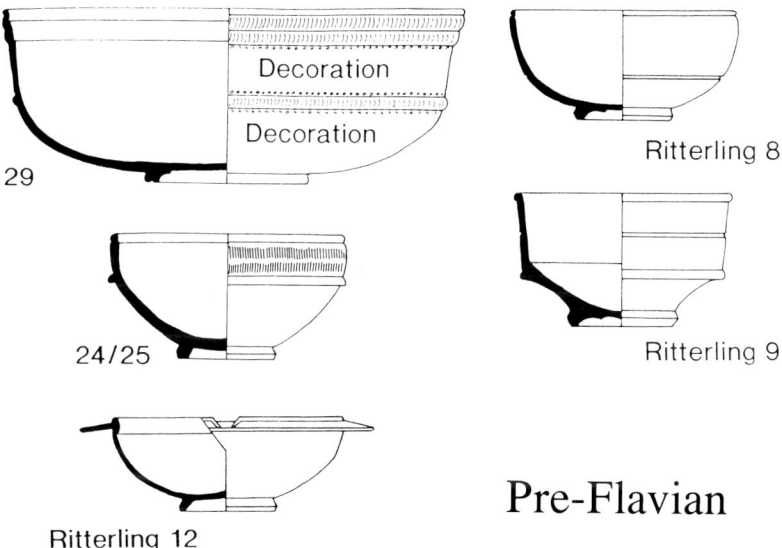

29

Decoration

Decoration

24/25

Ritterling 12

Ritterling 8

Ritterling 9

Pre-Flavian

Fig 68

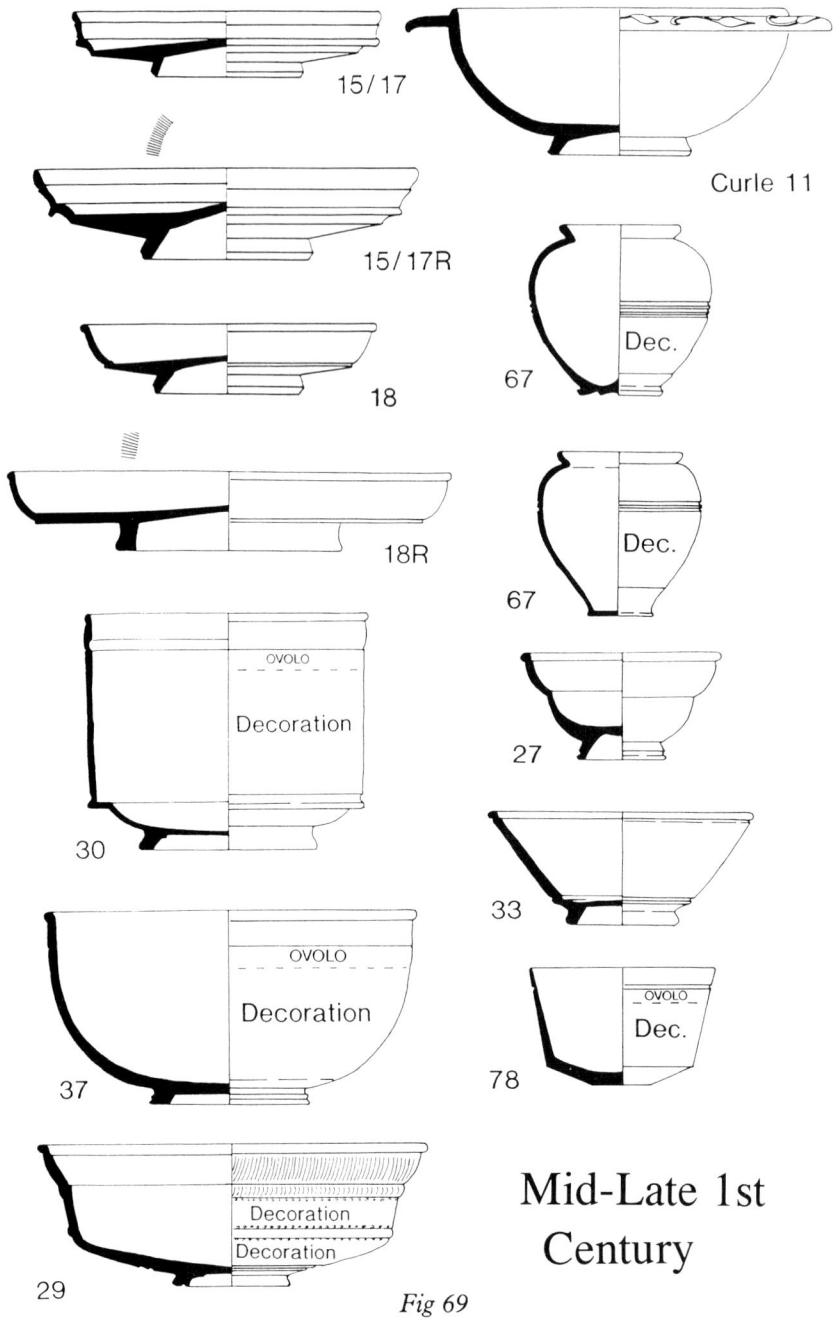

15/17

15/17R

18

18R

OVOLO

Decoration

30

OVOLO

Decoration

37

Decoration
Decoration

29

Curle 11

67 Dec.

67 Dec.

27

33

78 OVOLO Dec.

Mid-Late 1st Century

Fig 69

114

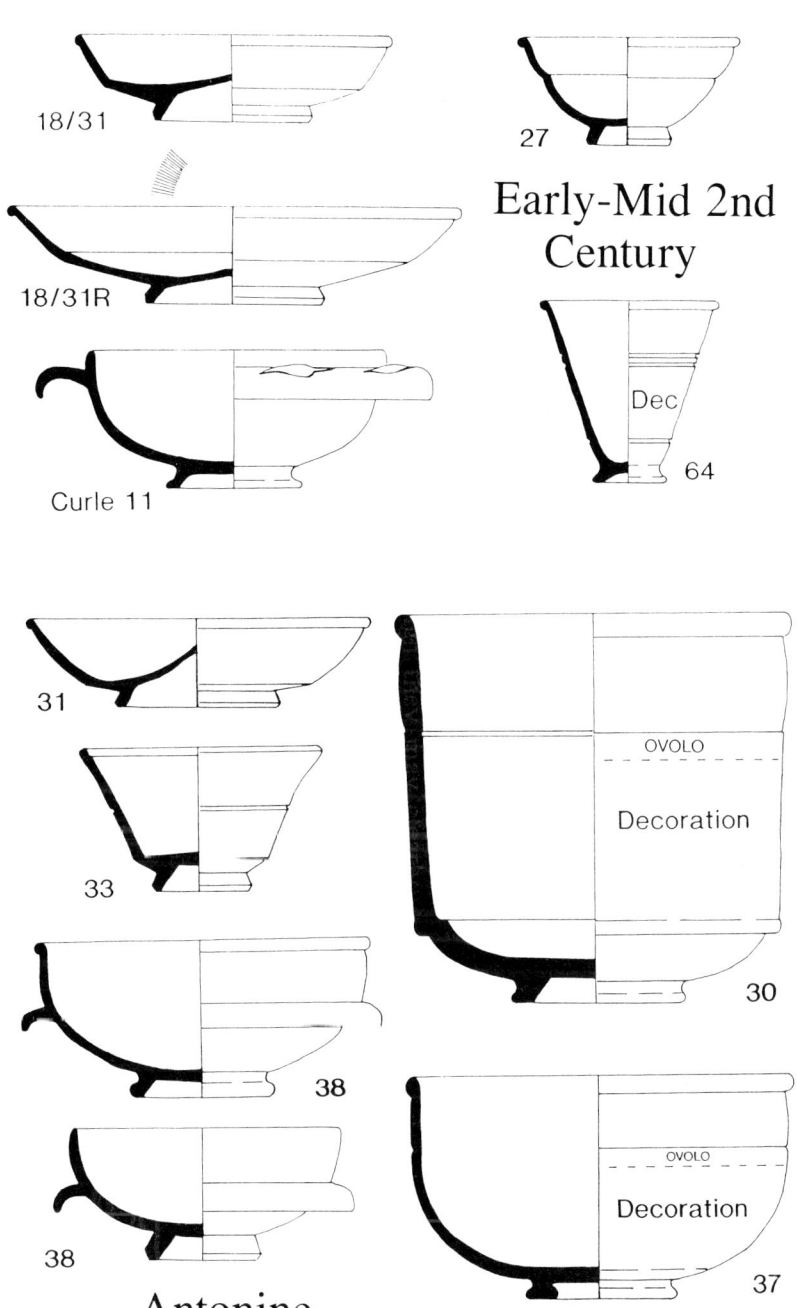

18/31

18/31R

Curle 11

27

Early-Mid 2nd Century

Dec

64

31

33

38

38

Antonine

OVOLO

Decoration

30

OVOLO

Decoration

37

Fig 70

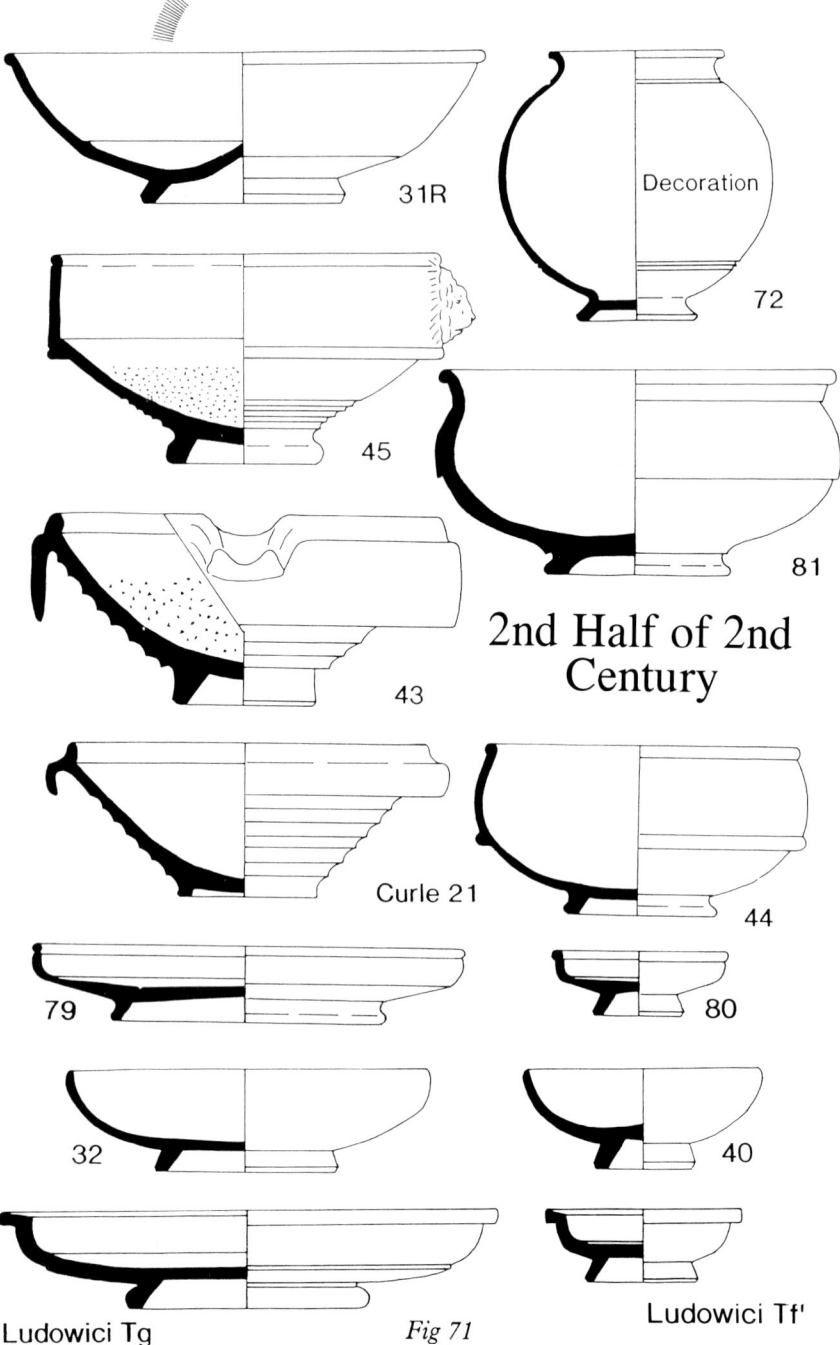

31R

Decoration

72

45

81

43

2nd Half of 2nd
Century

Curle 21

44

79

80

32

40

Ludowici Tg

Fig 71

Ludowici Tf'

116

Glossary

The terms used in samian reports are not always immediately intelligible to the nonspecialist reader. The list below is intended to explain some of the more common terms. It is also true that the terminology of reports is not entirely uniform and, simply by providing a glossary, it is hoped to standardize usage. *Illustrations of individual details below are at 1:1; larger designs are at 1:2. They always appear below their descriptions.*

Ante Cocturam
'Before firing'. The term is generally used of graffiti or signatures scratched in the mould before firing. In theory, the passage of a point across the unfired clay will throw up slight ridges at either side of the groove and these will be visible in the resultant pot. In practice, such slight evidence is not easy to spot.

Anthemion
The term is derived from architectural usage, where it is applied to honeysuckle or palmette ornament often found on cornices and on Ionic capitals. It is also much used by historians of interior decoration to describe motifs resembling the flower of the honeysuckle found in neo-classical decor. The numerous editions of Banister Fletcher's, *A History of Architecture*, define architectural usage (in a Glossary) and illustrate examples. In view of the wide variation of possible motifs the term is probably best avoided.

Arcade
A design divided by vertical borders linked by semi-circular 'arches' (often festoons or half-medallions impressed rounded side upwards).

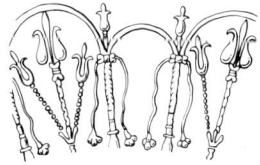

Astragalus
A 'bolster' of bead and reel. As an isolated design an astragalus is generally found as a sequence either of reel, bead and reel, or of double reel, bead and double reel.

Astragalus Border

A continuous border of bead and reel usually as a simple bead-reel-bead-reel sequence. Found on some Central Gaulish designs.

Barbotine

Decoration in soft clay or slip trailed on to the surface of the pot when dried (presumably to a leather-hard state). Sometimes vessels with spouts were used for trailing, but the effect is much as that achieved when decorating a cake with the aid of an icing bag. The term is sometimes used in its anglicized form (barbotine), sometimes in its French form (*en barbotine*).

Basal Wreath

A continuous design, not, as the name might suggest, on the base, but at the base of the decoration, often in the form of a wreath (qv) of leaves or chevrons.

Beaded Border

A border consisting of a row of small dots (= beads) usually used to divide panels or zones within a design.

Bifid

Properly used as an adjective, usually in connection with a double-leaf ornament, but occasionally used as a noun in the same context. Sometimes the term *bilobed* is used as an alternative.

Block

A rectangular panel totally filled with a repeating, usually small design such as leaf tips. Blocks generally act as spacers in a panel design.

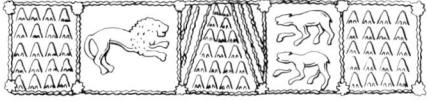

Border

A linear feature (usually a wavy line or bead row) used to divide elements in the design (eg one panel from another or the ovolo or basal wreath from the main design).

Bottle Bud

A curved bud, often with leaves above, looking something like a rose-hip or a 'stretched' pomegranate.

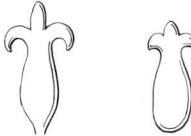

Carination

A sharp change of direction in the profile of a vessel. Such a change frequently occurs between the two zones of decoration on form 29.

Chevron

A V-shaped ornament, usually arranged in a series and placed either vertically or horizontally.

Cordate

A heart-shaped motif, usually a leaf or bud.

En Barbotine
See barbotine.

Festoon

A motif consisting of an approximately semi-circular border, 'hanging' downwards in continuous series. Usually festoons contain subsidiary motifs within the lobes thus formed. See also *arcade*.

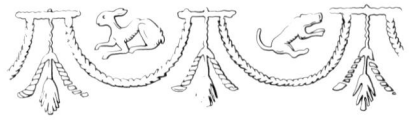 

Free-Style

A continuous design, usually with figures, which runs around the whole pot, without rigid divisions.

Gadroon

(Sometimes 'godroon'). A repeating fluted design, usually in the lower part of the pot (often the lower zone of form 29). Gadroons are often straight, but S-shaped (or rounded Z-shaped) gadroons are possible. Cf *volutes*.

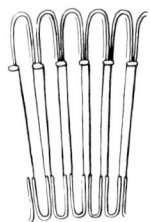  

Infilled Scroll

A scroll (qv) with the upper or lower lobe totally filled with a repetitive design such as leaf tips.

Inhabited Scroll

A scroll design containing figures in the upper or lower lobe (or in both lobes). See *scroll*.

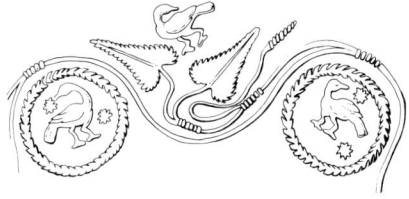

Lanceolate

The adjective is usually used in connection with leaves or buds. Although it could be used for any pointed leaf or bud, those thus described are generally spear-like or pointed-spade-like in appearance.

Medallion

A circular frame, usually of one or more ridges, but sometimes more wreath-like in design. Medallions are usually large enough to enclose smaller motifs.

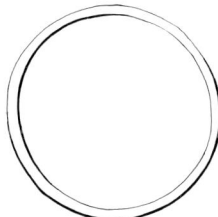 

Nautilus

See *volute*.

Ovolo

The term 'egg-and-dart' or 'egg-and-tongue' is more self explanatory but is rarely used in samian reports. The ovolo is most commonly used as the upper border of designs on forms 30 and 37. See also *tongue*.

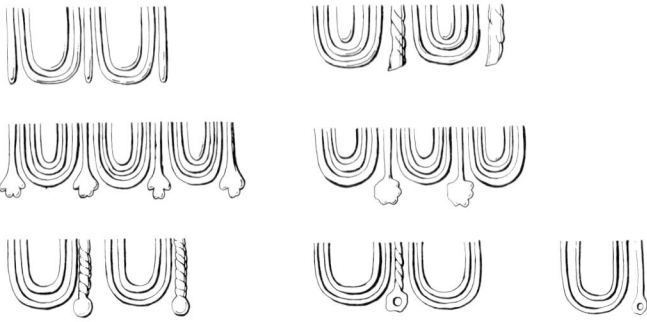

Palisade

A series of upright, often pointed motifs arranged point upwards as in a fence.

Poinçon

A hand-stamp used to impress individual motifs into the mould. It is also used for the name-stamps impressed into the mould or into the finished vessel. See p 5.

Post Cocturam

'After firing'. Usually used in connection with graffiti or signatures written in a mould after it was fired. In theory, the passage of a point across fired clay should result in chipping and splintering of the surface such as will be visible on the resultant pot. In practice, such slight evidence is not easy to spot. Cf *ante cocturam*.

Roped

The term is usually used for borders of elongated beads arranged diagonally to resemble a rope.

Saltire

A diagonal (or 'St Andrew's') cross. The term is usually used to describe quite elaborate panels based upon such a cross.

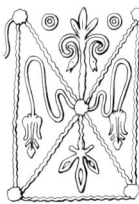 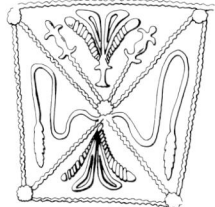

Scroll

An undulating design, usually of vegetation. The large wavy line of the main framework of the design produces upper and lower lobes which attract other motifs. See *inhabited scroll* and *infilled scroll*.

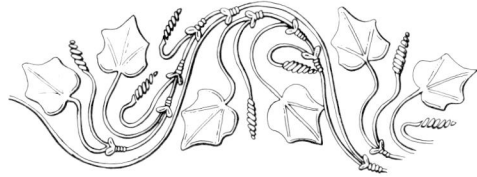 

Spiral

A term often used for what might more accurately be described as half a curly S placed at a variety of angles. Some spirals (such as our right hand example) will have been drawn freehand into the mould.

Stirrup Leaf

A composite design most common on South Gaulish pieces and consisting of one or more curling thin leaves joined to a lanceolate (spear- or spade-shaped) leaf and generally with smaller leaves arranged tassel-like behind the point of junction.

Tongue

Used of the tongue or dart in ovolo (egg-and-tongue) decoration (qv). The tongue can be plain or have a variety of small ornamental lower ends thus giving it tassel or pendant appearance. In some, mainly pre-Flavian, examples, rosettes are found added freehand to plain tongues instead of being carved with them as a single *poinçon*.

Trident

The term is self-explanatory. Usage is usually in connection with the triple ends of ovolo tongues and other small motifs.

Trifid

Usually used of stylised leaves arranged in threes, either as single ornaments or as the basic element of a wreath. See *bifid*.

Tulip

The term is sometimes used of buds or leaves with a vaguely tulip-like appearance.

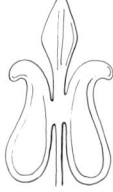

Twist

This convenient term is used by Stanfield & Simpson to describe a cigar-shaped ornament usually with striations. It can also be used of the interlocking ?bows used by a few Central Gaulish potters (eg Advocisus as illustrated here).

Volute

The term is used for curved elongated S-shaped motifs which are generally elaborate and have a certain resemblance to sea creatures such as the *nautilus*. Volutes are generally found as part of a repeating design around the lower half of vessels (usually the lower zones of form 29).

Winding Scroll

An alternative name for a scroll (qv).

Wreath

A repeating, usually vegetative motif arranged to run around the vessel in a straight line. When a wreath occurs at the bottom of a design scheme, it is usually called a *basal wreath* (qv).

 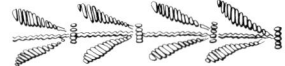

Zonal

A design which is divided by a series of continuous horizontal borders running right round the pot is called a zonal design. Form 29 was divided by its carination into upper and lower zones. Such designs were inherited by early form 37s and so zonal design was particularly popular on 37 during this early period in its history but can appear comparatively frequently down to the Hadrianic period.

Bibliography

Anderson, A C, & Anderson, A S, (eds) 1981 Roman pottery research in Britain and north-west Europe, *BAR Int ser* **123**, Oxford.

Atkinson, D, 1914 A hoard of samian ware from Pompeii, *J Roman Studies*, **4** 26–64.

——————, 1942 *Report on the excavations at Wroxeter (the Roman city of Viroconium) in the County of Salop, 1923–27*, Birmingham.

Bédoyère, G de la, 1988 *Samian Ware*, Princes Risborough.

Bémont, C, 1977 Moule de gobelets ornés de la Gaule centrale au Musée des Antiquités nationales, 33rd supplement to *Gallia*, Paris.

——————, & Jacob, J P, 1986 *La terre sigillée gallo-romaine*, Documents d'Archéologie Française, No 6, Paris.

Bennett, J, 1978 A further vessel by the Aldgate-Pulborough Potter, *Britannia*, **9** 307–13.

Bernhard, H, 1981 Zur diskussion um die chronologie Rheinzaberner Relieftöpfer, *Germania*, **59** 79–93.

Bird, J, 1977 African red slip ware in Roman Britain in J Dore & K Greene, (eds) *Roman pottery studies in Britain and beyond, BAR suppl series* **30**, Oxford, 269–77.

——————, 1986 Samian wares, in L Miller, J Schofield, & M Rhodes, *The Roman quay at St Magnus House, London*, London & Middlesex Arch Soc Special Paper **8** 139–85.

——————, 1993 3rd-century samian ware in Britain, *J Roman Pottery Studies*, **6**, 1–14

Bittner, F K, 1986 Zur Forsetzung der Diskussion um die Chronologie der Rheinzaberner Relieftöpfer, *Bayerische Vorgeschichtsblätter*, **51** 233–59.

Bulmer, M, 1980 An introduction to Roman samian ware, Chester (reprinted from *J Chester Arch Soc*, **62** [1979]).

Bushe-Fox, 1926 *First report on the excavation of the Roman fort at Richborough, Kent, Rep Res Comm Soc Antiq London*, **6**.

——————, 1928 *Second report on the excavations of the Roman fort at Richborough, Kent, Rep Res Comm Soc Antiq London*, **7**.

——————, 1932 *Third report on the excavations of the Roman fort at Richborough, Kent, Rep Res Comm Soc Antiq London*, **10**.

——————, 1949 *Fourth report on the excavations of the Roman fort at Richborough, Kent, Rep Res Comm Soc Antiq London*, **16**.

Chenet, C, & Gaudron, G, 1955 La céramique sigillée d'Argonne des IIe et IIIe siècles, 6th supplement to *Gallia*, Paris.

Cunliffe, B, 1968 *Fifth report on the excavations of the Roman fort at Richborough, Kent, Rep Res Comm Soc Antiq London*, **23**.

——————, 1971 *Excavations at Fishbourne, 1961–9, Vol II, the finds, Rep Res Comm Soc Antiq London*, **26**.

Curle, J, 1911 *A Roman frontier post and its people. The fort of Newstead in the parish of Melrose*, Glasgow.

Czysz, W, 1982 Der Sigillata-Geschirrfund von Cambodunum-Kempten. Ein Beitrag zur Technologie und Handelskunde mittelkaiserzeitlicher Keramik, *Bericht der Römisch-Germanische Kommission*, **63** 282–350.

Déchelette, F, 1904 *Les vases céramique ornés de la Gaule Romaine. Tome 2.* Paris.

Delort, E, 1953 *Vases ornées de la Moselle*, Nancy.

Edwards, B J N, & Webster, P V, 1985 *Ribchester Excavations. Part 1. Excavations in the Roman Fort*, Cardiff.

——————, & ——————, 1988 *Ribchester Excavations. Part 3. Excavations in the Civil Settlement. B Pottery and Coins*, Cardiff.

Ettlinger, E, Hedinger, B, Hoffmann, B, Kendrick, P, Pucci, G, Roth-Rubi, K, Scheider, G, von Schnurbein, S, Well, C, & Zabehlicky-Scheffenegger, S, 1990 *Conspectus formarum terrae sigillatae italico modo confectae*, Bonn.

Fiches, J L, Guy, M, & Poncin, L, 1978 Un lot de vases sigillés des premieres années du règne de Neron dans l'un des ports de Narbone, *Archaeonautica*, **2** 185–219.

Fischer, C, 1969 *Die Terra Sigillata-Manufaktur von Sinzig am Rhein*, Rheinische Ausgrabungen, Band 5, Dusseldorf.

Folzer, E, 1913 *Die Bilderschüsseln der ostgallischen Sigillata-Manufacturen*, Bonn.

Forrer, R, 1911 *Die römischen Sigillata-Töpferein von Heilingenberg-Dinsheim und Ittenweiler im Elsass*, Stuttgart.

Frere, S, 1972 *Verulamium Excavations. Vol I, Rep Res Comm Soc Antiq London*, **28**.

——————, 1982 The Bignor villa, *Britannia*, **13** 135–96.

——————, 1984 *Verulamium Excavations. Vol III, Oxford Univ Comm for Arch Monogr* **1**, Oxford.

Gose, E, 1984 *Gefässtypen der römischen Keramik im Rheinland*, 4th Edition (of a work originally published in 1950 as Beiheft 1 of *Bonner Jahrbücher*, Kevelaer for Rheinisches Landesmuseum, Bonn), Köln.

Greene, K, 1992 *Roman Pottery*, London.

Grimes, W F, 1930 *Holt, Denbighshire. The works depot of the Twentieth Legion at Castle Lyons*, London. Also published as *Y Cymmrodor*, **41**.

Haalebos, J, 1977 Zwammerdam – Nigrum Pullum. Ein Auxiliarkastell am Niedergermanischen Limes, *Cingula*, **3**.

Haalebos, K, Mees, A, & Polak, M, 1991 Über Töpfer und Fabriken verzierter Terrasigillata des ersten Jahrhunderts, *Archäologisches Korrespondenzblatt*, **21** 79–91.

Hartley, B R, 1969 Samian ware or Terra Sigillata, in R G Collingwood, & I A Richmond, *The archaeology of Roman Britain*, 235–51 London. Reprinted as *Roman samian ware (Terra Sigillata)*, Herts Arch Soc 1970.

——————, 1972 The Roman occupation of Scotland: the evidence of the samian ware, *Britannia*, **3** 1–55.

——————, 1985 The samian ware, in L F Pitts, & J K St Joseph, *Inchtuthil. The Roman Legionary Fortress, Britannia Monographs*, **6**, 314–22 London.

Hawkes, C, & Hull, M R, 1947 *Camulodunum, Rep Res Comm Soc Antiq London*, **14**.

Hayes, J W, 1972 *Late Roman Pottery*, British School at Rome, London.

——————, 1980 *Supplement to Late Roman Pottery*, British School at Rome, London.

Hofmann, B, 1988 *L'Atelier de Banassac*, Revue Archéologiques Sites, Horssérié **33**, Gonfaron.

Holbrook, N, & Bidwell, P T, 1991 *Roman Finds from Exeter, Exeter Archaeological Reports: Volume 4*, Exeter.

Hermet, F, 1934 *La Graufesenque (Condatomago)*, Paris. (Reprinted, Marseille 1979).

Hulde-Zetsche, I, 1971 Glatte Sigillaten des 'Massenfundes' aus Trier, *Rei Cretariae Romanae Fautorum Acta*, **XIII** 21–39.

——————, 1972 *Trierer Reliefsigillata. Werkstatt I*. Frankfurt-am-Main.

——————, 1993 *Trierer Reliefsigillata Werkstatt II*, Bonn.

Hull, M R, 1958 *Roman Colchester, Rep Res Comm Soc Antiq London*, **20**.

Jacobs, J, 1912 Sigillatafunde aus einen römische Keller zu Bregenz, *Jahrbuch für Altertumskunde*, **6** 172–84, Taf I-V.

Johns, C, 1977 *Arretine and samian pottery*, reprinted with revisions, British Museum, London.

Karnitsch, P, 1955 *Die verzierte sigillata von Lauriacum (Lorch-Enns), Forschungen in Lauriacum*, **3**, Linz.

——————, 1959 *Die Reliefsigillata von Ovilava*, Linz.

Knorr, R, 1905 *Die verzierten Terra Sigillata Gefässe von Cannstatt und Köngen-Grinario*, Stuttgart.

—————, 1907 *Die verzierten Terra-Sigillata-Gefässe von Rottweil*, Stuttgart.

—————, 1912 *Südgallische Terra-Sigillata-Gefässe von Rottweil*, Stuttgart.

—————, 1919 *Töpfer und Fabriken verzierter Terra-Sigillata des ersten Jahrhunderts*, Stuttgart.

—————, 1952 *Terra-Sigillata-Gefässe des ersten Jahrhunderts mit Töpfernamen*, Stuttgart.

—————, & Sprater, F, 1927 *Die westpfalzischen Sigillata-Töpfereien von Blickweiler und Eschweilerhof*, Speier.

Labrousse, M, 1975 Céramiques et potiers de Montans, *Les dosiers de l'archéologie*, 9 59–70.

Lerat, L, & Jeannin, Y, 1960 Les céramique sigillée de Luxeuil, *Annales Litteraires de l'Université de Besançon*, 31.

Ludowici, W, 1908 *Katalog III: Urnengräber römischer Töpfer in Rheinzabern*, Munich.

—————, 1912 *Katalog IV: Römische Ziegel-Gräber*, Munich.

—————, 1927 *Katalog V: Stempel Namen und Bilder römischer Töpfer aus meinen Ausgrabungen in Rheinzabern, 1901–14*.

—————, & Ricken, H, 1948 *Die Bilderschüsseln der römischen Töpfer von Rheinzabern (Tafelband)*, *Ludowici Katalog VI*, Speyer 1948.

Lutz, M, 1970 *L'Atelier de Saturninus et de Satto à Mittelbronn (Moselle)*, 22nd supplement to *Gallia*, Paris.

—————, 1977 *La sigillée de Boucheporn (Moselle)*, 32nd supplement to *Gallia*, Paris.

Manning, W H, 1993 *Report on the excavations at Usk. The Roman Pottery*, Cardiff.

Marichal, R, 1988 *Les graffites de La Graufesenques*, 47th supplement to *Gallia*, Paris.

Marsh, G, 1979a Nineteenth and twentieth century antiquities dealers and Arretine ware from London, *Trans London & Middlesex Arch Soc*, 30 125–9.

—————, 1979b Three vessels by the Aldgate-Pulborough potter from London, *Trans London & Middlesex Arch Soc*, 30 185–7.

—————, 1981 London's samian supply and its relationship to the Gallic samian industry, *Anderson & Anderson* 173–238.

Martin, T, 1974 Deux années de recherches archéologiques à Montans (Tarn), *Revue archéologique du Centre*, 13 123–43.

Mary, G, 1967 *Novaesium I. Die südgallische Terra-Sigillata aus Neuss*, *Limesforschungen*, Band 6, Berlin.

May, T, 1916 *The pottery found at Silchester*, Reading.

—————, 1930 *Catalogue of the Roman pottery in the Colchester and Essex Museum*, Cambridge.

—————, & Hope, L, 1917 Catalogue of the Roman pottery in the Museum, Tullie House, Carlisle, *Trans Cumberland & Westmorland Ant & Arch Soc*, New series, **17** 114–97.

McCarthy, M R, 1990 *A Roman, Anglian and Medieval site at Blackfriars Street, Carlisle. Excavations 1977–9, Cumberland & Westmorland Ant & Arch Soc Research Series No* **4**, Kendal.

Mees, A, 1990 Verzierte Terra Sigillata aus den Ausgrabungen bei Vechten in den Jahren 1920–1927, *Oudheidkundige Mededelingen uit het Rijksmuseum van Oudheden te Leiden*, **70** 109–81.

—————, 1993 Zur Gruppenbildung Rheinzaberner Modelhersteller und Ausformer, *Jahrsberichte aus Augst und Kaiseraugst*, **14** 227–55.

—————, 1995 *Modelsignierte Dekorationen auf südgallischer Terra Sigillata, Forschungen und Berichte zur Vor- und Frühgeschichte in Baden-Württemberg, Band* **54**, Stuttgart.

Monaghan, J, 1993 *Roman Pottery from the Fortress: 9 Blake Street, The Archaeology of York* **16**(7). CBA for York Archaeol Trust

Muller, G, 1968 *Das Lagerdorf des Kastells Butzbach. Die Reliefverzierte Terra Sigillata, Limesforschungen*, Band 5, Berlin.

Nash-Williams, V E, 1929 The Roman Legionary Fortress at Caerleon in Monmouthshire. Report on excavations carried out in 1926, *Archaeol Cambrensis*, **87** 237–307.

—————, 1932 The Roman legionary fortress at Caerleon...., the Prysg Field, 1927–9. Part III, *Archaeol Cambrensis*, **87** 265–349.

Niblett, R, 1985 *Sheepen: an early Roman industrial site at Camulodunum, CBA Res Rep* **57**, London.

Oelmann, F, 1914 *Die Keramik des Kastells Niederbieber*, Frankfurt am Main.

O & P *See Oswald & Pryce 1920*.

Orton, C, & Tyers, P, 1990 Slicing the pie – a framework for comparing ceramic assemblages, *Medieval Ceramics*, **14** 55–6.

Oswald, F, 1927 Cursive writing of Gaulish Potters, *J Roman Studies*, **17** 162–4 & Pls VI-IX.

—————, 1931 *Index of potters' stamps on terra sigillata, 'samian ware'*, published privately, Margidunum (East Bridgeford).

—————, 1936–7 *Index of figure types on terra sigillata, Univ of Liverpool, Annals of Arch & Anth supplement*.

—————, 1945 Decorated ware from Lavoye, *J Roman Studies*, **35** 49–57.

—————, & Pryce, T Davies, 1920 *An introduction to the study of terra sigillata*, London.

Perrin, J R, 1990 *Roman Pottery from the Colonia 2: General Accident and Rougier Street, The Archaeology of York* **16**(4), CBA for York Archaeol Trust.

Picon, M, 1973 *Introduction à l'étude technique des céramiques sigillées de Lezoux,* Centre de recherches sur les techniques greco-romaines, Dijon.

Picon, M, Vichy, M, & Meille, E, 1971 Composition of the Lezoux, Lyon and Arrezzo samian ware', *Archaeometry,* **13** 191–208.

Picon, M, Carré, C, Cordoliani, M L, & Vichy, M, 1975 Composition of the La Graufesenque, Banassac and Montans Terra Sigillata, *Archaeometry,* **17** 191–9.

Polak, M, 1988 Some observations on the production of Terra Sigillata at La Graufesenque, *Archäologisches Korrespondenzblatt,* **19** 145–54.

——————, 1993 Some observations on the chronology of form 29, *Annales de Pegasus 1990–1991,* 64–7.

Pryce, T Davies, & Oswald, F, 1928 Roman London: its initial occupation as evidenced by early types of Terra Sigillata, *Archaeologia,* **78** 73–110.

RCHM 1928 *An inventory of the historical monuments of London. Vol III. Roman London,* Royal Commission on Historical Monuments (England), London.

Ricken, H, 1934 Die Bilderschüsseln der Kastelle Saalburg und Zugmantel, *Saalburg Jahrbuch,* **8** 130–82, Taf VII-XIV.

——————, & Fischer, C, 1963 *Die Bilderschüsseln der römischen Töpfer von Rheinzabern (Textband),* Bonn.

Robertson, A, 1975 *Birrens (Blatobulgium),* Edinburgh.

Rogers, G, 1974 *Poteries sigillées de la Gaule Centrale. I. Les motifs non figurés,* 28th supplement to *Gallia,* Paris.

S&S, S&S 1990 *See Stanfield & Simpson 1958 and 1990.*

Schönberger, H, & Simon, H-G, 1966 *Novaesium II. Die Mittelkaiser zeitliche Terra Sigillata von Neuss, Limesforschungen,* Band 7, Berlin.

Simon, H-G, 1968 Das Kleinkastell Degerfeld in Butzbach, Kr. Friedbach (Hessen). Datierung und Funde, *Saalburg Jahrbuch,* **25** 5–64.

——————, & Kohler, H-J, 1992 *Ein Geschirrdepot des 3. Jahrhunderts. Grabungen im Lagerdorf des Kastells Langenhain, Materialien zu römisch-germanischen Keramik* 11, Bonn.

Simpson, G, 1952 The Aldgate potter: a maker of Romano-British samian ware, *J Roman Studies,* **42** 68–71.

——————, 1976 Decorated terra sigillata at Montans, *Britannia,* **7** 244–73.

——————, no date *The decorated samian ware from Central Gaul in the British Museum.* A typescript catalogue deposited in the Library of the Society of Antiquaries of London.

——————, & Rogers, G, 1969 Cinnamus de Lezoux et quelques potiers contemporains, *Gallia,* **27** 3–14.

Smith, R, 1907 The wreck on Pudding Pan Rock, Herne Bay, Kent, *Proc Soc of Ant of London,* 2nd series, (1905–7) **21** 268–92.

——————, 1909 The diving operations on Pudding Pan Rock, Herne Bay, Kent and... the Gallo-Roman red ware recently discovered, *Proc Soc of Ant of London*, 2nd series, **22** (1907–9) 395–414.

Stanfield, J, 1929 Unusual forms of terra sigillata, *Archaeol J*, **86** 113–51.

——————, 1936 Unusual forms of terra sigillata: second series, *Archaeol J*, **93** 101–16.

——————, 1937 Romano-Gaulish decorated jugs and the work of the potter Sabinus, *J Roman Studies*, **27** 168–79 & pl XXI–XXIV.

Stanfield, J, & Simpson, G, 1958 *Central Gaulish Potters*, Oxford for Durham.

——————, & ——————, 1990 *Les potiers de la Gaule Centrale*, Revue Archéologiques Sites, Hors-série no **37**, Gonfaron.

Storey J M V, Symonds R P, Hart F A, Smith D M, & Walsh J N, 1989 A chemical investigation of 'Colchester' samian by means of inductively-coupled plasma emission spectrometry, *J Roman Pottery Studies*, **2** 33–43.

Taylor, J, 1991 *The Roman Pottery from Castle Street, Carlisle: Excavations 1981–2, Cumberland & Westmorland Ant & Arch Soc Research Series*, No 5, Fascicule 5 (available as a separately printed fascicule and also on microfiche as part of the complete Research Series volume, M R McCarthy, *The Roman Waterlogged Remains and later features at Castle Street, Carlisle: Excavations 1981–2).*

Terrisse, J, 1968 *Les céramiques sigillées gallo-romaines des Martres-de-Veyre*, 19th supplement to *Gallia*, Paris.

Vanderhoeven, M, 1974–8 *Funde aus Asciburgium. Heft 2–3 (1974). Heft 5–7 (1975, 1976, 1978)*, Duisburg und Rheinhausen. Heft 2 deals with Central and East Gaulish wares, Heft 3 with stamps and Heft 5–7 with South Gaulish pottery.

Vernhet, A, 1976 Creation Flavienne de six services de vaiselle à La Graufesenque, *Figlina* **1** 13–27.

——————, 1981 Un four de La Graufesenque (Aveyron): la cuisson des vases sigillés, *Gallia* **39** 26–43.

Wacher, J, & McWhirr, A, 1982 *Cirencester Excavations I. Early Occupation at Cirencester*, Cirencester.

Walke, N, 1965 *Das römische Donaukastell Straubing-Sorviodunum*, Limesforschungen Band 3, Berlin.

Walters, H, 1908 *Catalogue of the Roman pottery in the Departments of Antiquities, British Museum*, London.

Webster, P, 1975 More British samian by the Aldgate-Pulborough potter, *Britannia*, **6** 163–70.

——————, 1981 The feeding cup: an unusual samian form, *Anderson & Anderson 1981*, 249–256.

—————, 1987 *Roman samian ware. Background notes,* Cardiff.

Wheeler, R E M, 1926 *The Roman fort near Brecon,* London.

—————, 1930 *London in Roman times,* London Museum Catalogue no 3.

Wild, F C, 1971 The samian ware, 53–66 in G D B Jones, Excavations at Northwich (Condate), *Arch J* **128** 31–77.

Young, C G, 1977 *Oxfordshire Roman Pottery, BAR Brit ser* **43**, Oxford.

Zienkiewicz, J D, 1993 Excavations in the *scamnum tribunorum* at Caerleon: the Legionary Museum site 1983–5, *Britannia* **24** 27–140 (samian 87–98).

Index by L Adkins

Page numbers in bold represent the main references. Numbers in italics represent the pages on which figures occur.